THE IDEA OF PERSONALITY IN SUFISM

THE IDEA OF PERSONALITY IN SUFISM

REYNOLD ALLEYNE NICHOLSON

GYAN

Published by

GYAN

Gyan Publishing House
5, Ansari Road
Daryaganj, New Delhi-110002
Phone: 011-47034999, 9811692060
E-mail: books@gyanbooks.com

Distribution Network
gyanbooks.com
India, USA, Canada, UK, Australia

ISBN: 978-93-7225-421-1 (PB)

First Published, 1935

2nd Impression 2026

Printed at: Gyan Press, Delhi.

THE IDEA OF PERSONALITY IN SUFISM
Author: REYNOLD ALLEYNE NICHOLSON

THE IDEA OF PERSONALITY IN ṢUFISM

BY

REYNOLD A. NICHOLSON
LITT.D., LL.D., F.B.A.

IDARAH-I ADABIYAT-I DELLI
2009, QASIMJAN STREET. DELHI-6

PREFACE

EXCEPTING a few verbal changes and the addition of footnotes, these lectures appear in the form in which they were delivered at the School of Oriental Studies last summer. As they owe their existence to my old friend D. B. Macdonald, I hope he will pardon me for dedicating them to him, though he, no doubt, would have handled the subject in a different way and would have done full justice to some aspects of it which I have passed over lightly. Where so much turns on difficult questions of interpretation, I could only state the general conclusions and give a broad view of the evidence supporting them. My chief purpose was to show, by means of examples chosen from the literature, that Ṣúfism is not necessarily pantheistic but often bears the marks of a genuine personal religion inspired by a personal God, even if we must beware of attributing to Moslems all that the term "personality" suggests to us.

REYNOLD A. NICHOLSON.

CAMBRIDGE,
December, 1922.

TO

DUNCAN B. MACDONALD

اذا كانت الضمائر مؤتلفه، لم يضرها أن تكون
الديار مختلفه.

This definition will provide a convenient starting-point for our discussion. I do not suppose that it would satisfy Moslem theologians. For in a well-known article of their creed it is laid down that Allah is entirely different from all created beings, and we know personal relations to be impossible without some element of likeness, without some degree of moral affinity. And further, although the criterion suggested by Professor Webb, whereby we should decide whether the relation is personal or not, would present no difficulty to Moslems—they have terms equivalent to transcendence and immanence in their own theology—few of them, I think, would be prepared to deny personality to a God either so immanent or so transcendent that personal relations with Him are, to us, barely conceivable. While in Islam as elsewhere personal religious experience is not peculiar to the mystics, it can hardly rise to its full height without becoming mystical, and this is the case in Islam to a greater extent than in Christianity. The point of view from which the subject is here regarded has, I hope, been made clear, but only a very imperfect sketch can be attempted on the present occasion. It will be my aim to bring before you, in historical order so far as possible, some of the ways in which earnestly religious Moslems have expressed and satisfied their craving for personal intercourse between themselves and God.

Apart from the fact that Ṣúfism, like every other religious movement in Islam, has its roots in the Koran and the Sunna and cannot be understood unless we study it from the source upwards, the particular aspect of it which we are now considering takes us back at once to the man with whom the Islamic idea of Divine personality begins and who himself during the Middle Ages became the object of a mystical devotion comparable to that which has often attached itself to the person of Christ. We must therefore spend a few moments on the problem of Mohammed's relation to God, leaving for a subsequent lecture the question why and how the view of the person of the Prophet which prevailed amongst his Moslem contemporaries was so fundamentally altered in after days, when Islam had spread beyond the borders of Arabia and grown into one of the great religions of the world.

I am going to take for granted what has often been doubted or denied—the sincerity of Mohammed and the reality of his prophetic inspiration—partly because it is a point on which all Moslems are agreed and also because it seems to me that on no other hypothesis can the origin and early history of Islam be accounted for. It is easy to emphasise the contradictions into which he was drawn by his postulate of a fixed and immutable revelation, written in a heavenly book and communicated to him by a process in which he was merely the passive medium, while the course of events constantly required that the revelation should be plastic and responsive to his needs. If he was an impostor, we can only wonder at his lack of foresight; but if he was sincere, it must be admitted that his prophetic endowment was not of the highest order. Had he stood in the same intimate and free relation to God as the Hebrew prophets, would it ever have occurred to him that the Koran is the literal Word of God, and would his own part in it have been confined to hearing it dictated by Gabriel? The stimulating thinker whose definition of personality I have quoted remarks that "the tendency of Islam is to reduce the personal relations which can exist between man and God to the lowest terms, to those, namely, which may exist between a slave and a master of absolutely unlimited power[1]." This statement would be better applied to the Koran than to Islam in general, and though it is a true statement as far as it goes, it gives no clue to the secret of Mohammed's enthusiasm. Few can read the short Súras, which stand last in the book but came first in order of time, without feeling that he was conscious of being, as we say, in touch with Allah—conscious, after much inward tribulation, that what possessed him was not an evil spirit but the spirit of Allah who by His grace had chosen him, like the prophets of old, to warn his countrymen of their impending doom "on the day when the earth shall be ground to dust, and thy Lord shall come, and the angels row by row; and Hell on that day shall be brought nigh" (Kor. LXXXIX, 22–24)[2]. The vision of Judgment stirred Mohammed to the depths of his soul, it broke down every barrier and set him face to face with the Lord who says, "Call unto Me and I will answer you" (Kor. XL, 62). So the Moslem "in prayer can come directly to God[3]." We see from the Koran that Mohammed spoke as a prophet, heedless of logical consistency. In him were two voices, one certainly louder and more frequent than the other, yet "each a mighty voice[4]." One voice declares that Allah sits on His throne, that He is the great Taskmaster whose eye is ever on His servants[5], as ready to punish

[1] Webb, *God and Personality*, p. 87.

[2] I follow Snouck Hurgronje and Andrae (*Die Person Muhammeds*, 8–10), who hold that what made Mohammed a prophet was his conviction that the Day of Judgment was at hand

[3] D. B. Macdonald, *The religious attitude and life in Islam*. p. 38

[4] Wordsworth, Sonnet entitled *Thought of a Briton on the Subjugation of Switzerland*.

[5] Kor. LXXXIX, 13.

and destroy the wicked as to pardon and protect the righteous; the other proclaims that Allah is the Reality (*al-Ḥaqq*)[1] which shall remain when all else has passed away[2], that He is the Light of heaven and earth[3], that He is nearer to us than our neck-vein[4], that wherever we turn He is present with us[5]. Is not this just what the Ṣúfís are never tired of saying? For them, indeed, Allah is pre-eminently the Beloved, while Mohammed's love of Him was overshadowed by his fear. Yet the former feeling was by no means strange to him. In a Súra of the Meccan period (LXXXV, 14) Allah is described as "the Loving One" (*al-Wadúd*); and in many passages it is affirmed that He loves the beneficent, the patient, those who keep themselves pure, and so on. Man's love of Allah is mentioned only thrice, but one of these references I must quote because it shows how closely Mohammed could identify himself with Allah; it has, too, a further significance which will appear when we come to consider the position occupied by the Prophet in Moslem theology. The passage runs thus (Kor. III, 29): "Say: if ye love Allah, follow me, so will Allah love you and forgive you your sins, for Allah is forgiving and merciful. Say: obey Allah and the Apostle" Here Mohammed seems to be echoing the words of Christ, "He that receiveth me receiveth him that sent me[6]"; "the Father himself loveth you because ye have loved me[7]." Be that as it may, there are many things in the Koran which afford a real basis for Ṣúfism. To express this fact in another way, though Mohammed's relation to God cannot on the whole be called one of intimacy, it had in it a mystical aspect,

[1] Kor. XXII, 6, 61, etc.
[2] Kor. XXVIII, 88; LV, 26–27.
[3] Kor XXIV, 35.
[4] Kor L, 15.
[5] Kor. II, 109.
[6] Matthew X, 40.
[7] John XVI, 27.

namely, a direct consciousness of the Divine presence, which is "religion in its most acute intense, and living stage[1]" Without that, I am convinced. he could never have become the founder of Islam.

When, after the Prophet's death, his followers established themselves in Persia, Syria, and Egypt, they were brought into contact with old religions, theologies and philosophies, under the influence of which their simple faith was gradually transformed. We can trace the working of these foreign ideas in every department of Moslem thought: in theology and jurisprudence no less than in asceticism and mysticism. Of course the foundation of the whole fabric was the Koran, a very quicksand of contradictory notions expressed in language that is often vague and obscure. The Koran, however, could be supplemented by the *Ḥadíth, i.e.* the Traditions of the Prophet. These were particularly useful for system-building just because they were so easy to invent: every student of Islam is aware how many sayings have been put in the Prophet's mouth by those who desired to claim Prophetic authority for their own doctrines. This pious fraud was practised by all the early Mohammedan sects. The Ṣúfís are not a sect, but they too produced a vast number of spurious Traditions to support their contention that Ṣúfism is in truth the esoteric teaching of the Prophet.

The oldest type of mysticism in Islam was ascetic and devotional rather than speculative, and the word "Ṣúfí" first appears in literature as a name applied to a certain class of ascetics[2]. In the second century of the Hijra there arose a spontaneous and wide-spread movement towards world-flight. Dreading the wrath to come, thou-

[1] Rufus Jones, *Studies in mystical religion*, Introd. p. xv.
[2] Jáḥiẓ, *Kitábu 'l-Bayán*, I, 138.

sands of men and women gave themselves up to the religious life, either singly or in companionship with a few friends. The consciousness of sin lay heavy on them: the slightest offence against the Law had to be expiated by a long penance. From the injunctions which they found in the Koran to think on God and trust in God they developed the practice of *dhikr* and the doctrine of *tawakkul*. Here, no doubt, they learned something from Christian asceticism. *Dhikr* was at first a form of meditation consisting in the incessant chanting of a brief litany such as "Allah! Allah!" "Subḥán Allah!" or the like. The command to trust in God (*tawakkul*) some of them carried out so thoroughly that they would not act on their own initiative at all, refusing, for example, to seek food or take medicine; and they scarcely exaggerate when they describe their attitude as that of a corpse in the hands of the washer who prepares it for burial. This kind of devotion might sink into lip-service and hypocrisy; still, for many of them, it was no matter of rule: it was as intensely real as the terrors which inspired it. Ḥasan of Baṣra, hearing mention made of the man who shall only be saved after having passed a thousand years in Hell-fire, burst into tears and exclaimed, "Oh, would that I were like that man![1]" And if in this emotional religion the master-feeling was fear, yet there was also love. With the growing influence of Hellenistic ideas Moslem asceticism became mystical: ascetic exercises began to be regarded, not as having their end in future salvation or perdition, but rather as a means of purifying the soul so that it may know and love God and attain to union with Him. As we have seen, the Koran speaks incidentally of God as loving men and of men as loving God, but the tone of

[1] *Qútu 'l-Qulúb*, I, 101.

these texts does not suggest that the Ṣúfí conception of Divine Love was derived from the Koran. Already in the second century after Mohammed the saintly woman, Rábi'a of Baṣra, implores God not to withhold from her the vision of His everlasting beauty[1], while Ma'rúf al-Karkhí, author of the earliest definition of Ṣúfism, declares that love is a gift of God and cannot be learned from men[2]. When Ma'rúf died, his pupil Sarí al-Saqaṭí saw him in a dream.

> Meseemed he was at the foot of God's throne, and God was saying to His angels, "Who is this?" They answered, "Thou knowest best, O Lord" Then God said to them, "This is Ma'rúf al-Karkhí, who was intoxicated with love of Me and will not recover his senses except by meeting Me face to face[3]"

That Ma'rúf felt himself to be in the closest personal communion with God appears from his saying on one occasion to Sarí al-Saqaṭí, "When you desire anything of God, adjure Him in my name[4]." According to the Egyptian Ṣúfí Dhu 'l-Nún (ob. A.H. 245 = A.D. 859), Divine Love is a mystery that must not be spoken of, lest it come to the ears of the vulgar[5]. Dhu 'l-Nún took a very important step in the development of Ṣúfism by distinguishing the mystic's knowledge of God (*ma'rifat*) from traditional or intellectual knowledge (*'ilm*) and by connecting the former with love of God (*maḥabbat*).

> "True knowledge of God," he says, "is not the knowledge that God is One, which is possessed by all believers; nor the knowledge of Him derived from proof and demonstration, which belongs to philosophers, rhetoricians, and theologians; but it is the knowledge of the attributes of Divine Unity,

[1] *Tadhkiratu 'l-Awliyá*, I, 73, 5.
[2] *Ibid.* I, 272, 12.
[3] Qushayrí (Cairo, 1318 A.H.), 11, 14.
[4] *Ibid* 11, 8.
[5] *Ibid* 173, 3 fr. foot.

which belongs to the Saints of God, those who behold God with their hearts in such wise that He reveals unto them what He revealeth not unto any one else in the world[1]."

And again: "Real knowledge is God's illumination of the heart with the pure radiance of knowledge," *i.e.* the sun can be seen only by the light of the sun[2]. Hence "the more a man knoweth God the deeper and greater his bewilderment in God," because (as the commentator explains) the nearer he is to the sun the more he is dazzled, until he reaches a point where he is not he[3].

"They that know God," Dhu 'l-Nún continues, "are not themselves and subsist not through themselves, but in so far as they are themselves they subsist through God. They move as God causes them to move, and their words are the words of God which roll upon their tongues, and their sight is the sight of God which hath entered their eyes. The Prophet, on whom be peace, told of these qualities when he related that God said. 'When I love a servant, I the Lord am his ear, so that he hears by Me, and his eye, so that he sees by Me, and his tongue, so that he speaks by Me, and his hand, so that he takes by Me[4].'"

These quotations show that what the Ṣúfís call *ma'rifat*, knowledge of God, resembles the γνῶσις of Hellenistic religion: it is an immediate experience in which the intellect has no share, an ecstatic contemplation of God by the divinely illuminated heart. Moreover, it involves the effacement of the individual self and the substitution of divine qualities for human; yet all this is the act of God. Just as St Paul said to his Galatian converts, "Now that ye have come to know God, or rather to be known of God[5]," so the Ṣúfí *'árif* or gnostic imputes all his knowledge to Him who by revealing Himself causes the veil

[1] *Tadhkiratu 'l-Awliyá*, I, 127, 3.
[2] *Ibid.* I, 127, 8.
[3] *Ibid* I, 127, 16.
[4] *Ibid.* I, 127, 21
[5] Galatians IV, 9.

of "otherness" and duality to disappear and the knower to be one with the known. And when Ṣúfís speak of knowing the unity of God, they mean no less than this. It was this doctrine of the Divine Unity that was taught in private by Junayd of Baghdád (ob. A.H 297 = A D. 909)[1]; and his pupil, the celebrated Ḥalláj, may have heard it from him.

The modern idea of Divine personality is derived from the doctrine of the Trinity, which, though it does not affirm the personality *of* God, affirms the existence of personal relations *in* His nature. Probably most of us would agree with Professor Webb, who thinks that, because "the Christian Church has worshipped as God a real historical person," it has been found easier in Christianity than elsewhere

> to secure what may be called "a personal religion" without a mystical dissipation of the personality of its Object, and to attribute personality to that Object without removing it to a distance from the worshipper too great to admit of genuine sympathy and devotion[2].

At any rate, those who hold such a view can find support for it in the history of Islam. For, in Islam, as I hope to show in my third Lecture, the strictly Unitarian doctrine, after having been worked out to the end, was met by the demands of the religious consciousness, which insisted on recognising the Logos in the person of Mohammed and went a long way towards identifying him with God. We shall examine that curious result of Moslem Unitarianism later on; meanwhile let us see in what fashion the orthodox creed was formulated.

In the Koran, for the most part, Allah is described as

[1] Qushayrí, 160, 14 and 22 *Kitáb al-Luma'*, 29

[2] Webb, *God and Personality*, p 81.

an infinitely transcendent Being who acts and feels like a human person. He can be pleased or displeased, besought, trusted, even loved: He has *religious* value. But Mohammed's conception was theologically indefensible. It had to be hardened into a dogmatic scheme, and the upshot may be stated in a few sentences culled from an authoritative article by Prof. D. B. Macdonald[1].

> "The situation," he says, "decreed that, more and more precisely, the starting-point should be the absolute unity, internal and external, of Allah and the representation of that unity as a tremendous will....Allah could suffer no change, could experience no emotions. Sorrow, pity, love, desire could have no part in him. When he acts, it is not because of any action or reaction of motives and purposes within him; it is by simple arbitrary will."

Then as to his nature, we cannot draw any conclusions from the qualities ascribed to him in the Koran.

> He may be called "Most Merciful" there, but that does not mean that he has a quality, Mercy, corresponding to anything in man. If he could be so described—that is, in similar terms with man—then he, too, would be a created being.

Further

> he creates us and he creates all that we do, immediately, directly, without any secondary causes....He is the only real agent in existence....It is open to Allah to do anything, to create good or evil, faith in one person and unbelief in another, knowledge in one and ignorance in another.... Every possible thing, even to the vague thoughts that suddenly rise in the mind, is controlled by Allah, by his Will and his Power.

A creed, fortunately, is not a religion. The devout Moslem keeps this Deity of dialectic well in the background. Yet He is always there and, as Professor Macdonald remarks,

[1] *Hartford Seminary Record*, vol. xx, No. 1 (1910), p. 21 foll.

may assert Himself at any time in an almost overwhelming way.

Ṣúfís, however, regard the Unity of God not as anything that can be apprehended by the intellect, but as a mystery that is revealed only to those whom God permits to realise it in their religious experience. We have seen that in order to love and know God the Ṣúfí must lose himself in the love and knowledge of God. Similarly, the *muwaḥḥid* or unifier of God cannot fully realise that God is One except by losing himself in the Oneness of God. Unification (*tawḥíd*) is defined as "the absoluteness of the Divine nature realised in the passing-away of the human nature[1]," so that "the man's last state reverts to his first state and he becomes even as he was before he existed[2]." That a doctrine of utter transcendence should lead straight to mystical union of the human personality with the divine was inevitable as soon as that doctrine stood opposed to a religion in which God is worshipped as the object of knowledge and love. The infinite distance between God and man God alone can annihilate; man has no power to bridge the chasm, therefore it is overleaped by a *tour de force* of the omnipotent Will. That idea lies behind the whole theory and practice of religious ecstasy on which the Ṣúfís throw so much stress. How should the mystic's conscious self not be obliterated and swept away by the transcendent glory of Him who in a sudden gleam reveals Himself as ineffably near? Must not the distinction of subject and object vanish altogether? For here God is all, and there is naught beside Him.

You will remember that we agreed to make the personality of God depend on the existence of personal

[1] *Kitáb al-Luma'*, 31 penult. [2] *Ibid.* 29, 11.

relations between Him and His worshippers, and also to treat such personal relations as incompatible either with a doctrine of extreme immanence or with a doctrine of extreme transcendence. Now in the early Ṣúfism of which I have been speaking we often find both these extremes in combination. Even Ḥalláj, who said *Ana 'l-Haqq*, "I am God," asserts in the strongest terms that God is transcendent and that the Creator must always remain other than the creature. There can be no doubt that the experience of *faná*, the passing-away of consciousness in mystical union, is consistent with belief in a personal God, though the same experience may equally well serve as a basis for pantheism when it is conceived as an end in itself, a Nirvâna in which the illusion of personality is extinguished for ever. That some Ṣúfís have so conceived it I am ready to admit. In the third century A.H. the negative doctrine of *faná* was taught by the famous Persian Ṣúfí, Báyazíd of Bisṭám, while the positive view—that the ultimate goal is not death to self (*faná*) but life in God (*baqá*)—was maintained by Abú Sa'íd al-Kharráz and since his time is often adopted by Ṣúfís who acknowledge the obligations of the Mohammedan religious law. It has been argued that Ṣúfism reaches its logical conclusion in the state of *faná* rather than in the succeeding state in which the mystic, having become endowed with Divine attributes, displays the Divine truth to mankind and fulfils the Divine Law in the world: this return from "intoxication" (*sukr*) to "sobriety" (*ṣaḥw*) is alleged to be a mere figment devised for the purpose of enabling Ṣúfís to pass for Moslems[1]. But Ṣúfism belongs to Islam just as much as Christian mysticism to Christianity, and no one can study it without frequently being

[1] R. Hartmann, *al-Ḳuschairîs Darstellung des Ṣûfîtums*, p. 93.

aware of a profound religious sentiment which seeks its final satisfaction, not in *denying* its own existence, but in *affirming* that it lives, moves, and has its being in the eternally active Will of Allah, and which, as a rule, expresses itself in language drawn from the closest form of *personal* relationship that we can imagine, namely, love. I have said that in this experience, uniting as it does the idea of Divine transcendence with the feeling of Divine immanence, there is an essential paradox. And we must note that each of the extremes approaches pantheism from an opposite direction. The pantheistic tendency in Ṣúfism is not wholly due to the feeling that God is one with His worshipper; it also proceeds from the notion of transcendence formulated in the scholastic-theological definition, according to which the absolute Will of Allah is the only real agent in the universe. But while the Ṣúfís no less than the Scholastics bring Islam to the verge of pantheism, Ṣúfism, unlike the system of Moslem theology, leaves room for personal religion. Only by ignoring the Fifty Articles of his creed can the Moslem come near to God; but the Ṣúfí who enjoys communion with God can, if he wishes, take the creed to his heart and see in its words a partial and inadequate reflection of what his inner light has revealed to him.

I will now illustrate some of the points in question from the great poem of Ibnu 'l-Fáriḍ, an Arabian mystic of the early 13th century—he was born at Cairo in A.D. 1182 and died there in A.D. 1235. During the interval of 300 years which divides him from the Ṣúfís with whom we have hitherto been concerned, much had happened of vital importance to the development of the doctrine and to the position of Ṣúfism within Islam. I shall come back to this in the next Lecture, which must give some account of the speculations of Ḥalláj and the life-work of Ghazálí. But Ibnu 'l-Fáriḍ is a more typical Ṣúfí than either of these, and by good luck he has left a unique record of his own mystical experiences, a *Pilgrim's Progress* in verse, composed in a style which is the very antithesis of Bunyan's—symbolical, exquisite, and curiously subtle. The poet writes from the level of one who has attained to *ittiḥád*, the state of permanent oneness with God. In the prelude, addressing a real or imaginary disciple, he recalls an earlier time of spiritual ebb and flow, when his love was still imperfect, and how he sought to relieve his anguish by telling it to the Divine Beloved.

I told how I fared in my love of thee, not because impatience made me weary of my sufferings, but to assuage my grief.
'Tis good to show fortitude towards enemies, but in the presence of loved ones aught save weakness is unseemly.
The excellence of my patience keeps me from complaining, though if I complained to my enemies of what I feel, they would do away with my complaint
And the issue of my patience in loving thee is praiseworthy if I endure the sorrows thou layest on me, but if I endure to be separated from thee, it is not praiseworthy
Whatever woe befalls me is a favour, inasmuch as my purpose holds firm against breaking my vows;
So for every pain in love, when it arises from thee, I give thanks instead of complaining.
Ay, and if the agonies of passion do me despite, yet are they reckoned in love as a kindness;
And my unhappiness, nay, my tribulation, is a bounty when wrought by thee, and my raiment of hardship worn for thy sake is the most ample of felicities.

* * * * * *

For when one is snared by Beauty, methinks his soul (even) from the most delicious life is (gladly) rendered up to death.
A soul that thinks to meet with no suffering in love, when it addresses itself to love, is spurned[1].

[1] *Tá'iyyatu 'l-Kubrá, vv.* 42–59.

He assures the Beloved that his love for Her is unchangeable:

Mine is a noble soul—a soul that would not forget thee even though thou should'st offer it, on condition of forgetting thee, what is beyond its wishes;
A soul that would not let go the true love I bear, even though it were removed far (from thee) by scorn and absence and hatred and the cutting-off of hope.
I have no way of departing from my Way in love, and if ever I shall turn aside from it, I shall abandon my religion[1].

He then refers to a passage in the Koran (VII, 171), where it is written that God, having drawn forth from the loins of Adam all the future generations of mankind, said to them, *Alastu bi-rabbikum*, "Am I not your Lord?" and received the answer *Balà*, "Yea," which (according to the Ṣúfí interpretation) sealed the covenant of mutual love between God and His creatures. He gave this pledge, he says, before his soul was clothed in the shadow of his clay, and he has never been false to it. And swearing a most solemn oath by all Her attributes of beauty, majesty, and perfection, he speaks his last word:

Verily, thou art the desire of my heart, and the end of my search, and the goal of my aim, and my choice and my chosen[2].

The Beloved now answers him. She tells him, in effect, that his claim to love Her is presumptuous and insincere. His regard for Her is really self-regard, his love self-love. The true lover must die to self

Thou art sworn to love, but to love of self: amongst my proofs (of this) is the fact that thou sufferest one of thy attributes to remain in existence.
For thou lov'st me not, so long as thou hast not passed away

[1] *Tá'iyyatu 'l-Kubrá*, vv 62–64. [2] *Ibid.* v. 76

in me; and thou hast not passed away so long as my form is not seen within thee.

* * * * * *

Such is Love: unless thou die, thou wilt not win thy will of the Beloved in aught. Then choose death or leave my love alone![1]

In reply he protests that this death is his dearest wish and prays the Beloved to grant it, whatever pain it may cost.

I said to her, "My spirit is thine: 'tis for thee to take it." How should it be in my power?
I am not one that loathes to die in love—I am always true (to death). my nature refuses aught else.
What should I hope to be said of me except "Such a one died of love"? Who will ensure me of that (death)?—for it is that I seek[2].

You will observe how entirely *personal* is the tone of this. Yet there is no real intimacy: the relation remains one of transcendence. Union with God lies far beyond the reach of the self *per se*: it can be attained only through *faná*, when the self "passes away" from itself and by thus dying lives in God (*baqá*).

If she lets my blood be shed in love of her, yet hath she established my rank on the heights of glory and eminence.
By my life though I lose my life in exchange for her love, I am the gainer; and if she wastes away my heart, she will make it whole once more[3].

Faná is described as a process wherein the soul is stripped of all its desires, affections, and interests, so that in ceasing to will for itself it becomes an object of the Divine will, that is, the beloved of God; and that which loves it and which it loves is now its inward and real

[1] *Tá'iyyatu 'l-Kubrá*, *vv.* 98–102.
[2] *Ibid. vv.* 103–105.
[3] *Ibid. vv.* 120–121.

self, not the self that has "passed away." Thus the unified personality finds the subject and object of worship in itself:

> Both of us are a single worshipper who, in respect of the united state, bows himself to his own essence in every act of bowing
>
> None prayed to me but myself, nor did I pray to any one but myself in the performance of every genuflexion[1]

Ibnu 'l-Fárid distinguishes three modes of experience, which may be called respectively normal, abnormal, and supernormal Normal experience is the multiple, shifting, consciousness of ordinary men, abnormal experience is the loss of that consciousness in ecstasy, and supernormal experience is the higher, mystical, unified consciousness which may be the result of ecstasy To normal experience Ibnu 'l-Fárid gives the name of "sobriety" (*saḥw*), to abnormal or ecstatic experience the name of "intoxication" (*sukr*), and to supernormal experience the name of "the sobriety of union" (*saḥwu 'l-jam'*) or "the second sobriety" (*al-saḥw al-thání*). This last is necessarily preceded by "intoxication" but does not necessarily follow it. In most cases the mystic, as soon as his fit of ecstasy is over, returns to normal consciousness. On the other hand it sometimes, though rarely, happens that "intoxication" is succeeded by a conscious state of "sobriety" or, as we might say, mystical clairvoyance, in which the seer regards himself as united with God. According to Ibnu 'l-Fáriḍ, this is the supreme degree of oneness (*ittiḥád*), and he claims to possess it permanently. Thus the Ṣúfí in the first stage of his journey is aware of himself as an individual distinct from God; in the second stage every distinction between Creator and creature has vanished,

[1] *Tá'iyyatu 'l-Kubrá, vv.* 153–154

and in the third stage he is aware of himself as being one with the Creator from whom he, as a creature, is distinct. While during the momentary "intoxication" of *faná* all the attributes of the self are negated, in "the sobriety of union" they are restored "with an increase," as the poet says, *i.e.* they are transmuted and wholly spiritualised. Therefore the highest mystical experience is positive and active in the sense that he who has reached it not only manifests the Divine attributes and actions in himself to others, but maintains a personal relation to the God with whom he is one and who nevertheless transcends him.

> And through her, not through myself, I began to guide unto her those who by themselves had lost the right ways; and 'twas she that (really) guided them[1].

It is true that Ibnu 'l-Fárid uses what may seem to us pantheistic language to express his feeling of oneness with God and dwells on the aspect of immanence far more than on the aspect of transcendence. A few verses will make this clear.

> When it (my essence) is not called "two," my attributes are hers, and since we are one, her outward aspect is mine.
> If she be called, 'tis I who answer, and if I am summoned she answers him who calls me and cries "*Labbayk!*" ("At thy service!").
> And if she speak, 'tis I who converse. Likewise, if I tell a story, 'tis she that tells it.
> The pronoun of the second person has gone out of use between us, and by its removal I am raised above the sect who separate[2].

"The sect who separate" are those who look at things from the standpoint of duality as opposed to unity, so that, for example, they regard their acts of worship as

[1] *Tá'iyyatu 'l-Kubrá, v.* 174. [2] *Ibid. vv.* 215–218.

proceeding from themselves, not as being done by God in them. But here the poet hardly goes beyond the orthodox doctrine of Islamic monotheism, that God is the only real agent in existence, a doctrine which is saved from being pantheistic by nothing else than its representation of God as a personal creative Will. And this, I believe, was essentially the position of Ibnu 'l-Fáriḍ, though in mystical fashion he identifies himself with that Will in all its manifestations.

None lives but his life is from mine, and every willing soul is obedient to my will;
And there is no speaker but tells his tale with my words, nor any seer but sees with the sight of mine eye;
And no silent listener but hears with my hearing, nor any one that grasps but with my strength and might;
And in the whole creation there is none save me that speaks or sees or hears[1].

In these lines Ibnu 'l-Fáriḍ is supposed to make himself one with Mohammed. At present it need only be said that according to the later Ṣúfís union with the Spirit of Mohammed signifies a relation to God somewhat like the relation to Him which by the Christian Fathers of Alexandria was thought to be implied in union with the Logos.

Some Mohammedan commentators who wrote under the influence of Ibnu 'l-'Arabí have treated the poem as the work of a pantheist belonging to the same school as themselves, and a recent Italian translator takes this view of it. In my opinion, both the internal and the external evidence is against the pantheistic interpretation. I cannot go into details here, but I have no doubt that what Ibnu 'l-Fáriḍ describes, or attempts to describe, is a personal religious experience of the most intimate kind. Just for that reason the poem has great

[1] *Tá'iyyatu 'l-Kubrá*, vv. 639–642.

psychological interest for students of Ṣúfism. It shows to us the full inner meaning of the Ṣúfí definition of *tawḥíd* (the Divine Unity) which has been quoted above—"the absoluteness of the Divine nature realised in the passing-away of the human nature." Ibnu 'l-Fáriḍ's *ittiḥád* is the mystical realisation of the idea of God that was developed by Moslem Unitarianism and set forth in the orthodox creeds. Unless I am mistaken, much of the so-called "pantheism" with which the Ṣúfís are often discredited is really founded on personal experience of the immanent and transcendent Unity of Allah. Though nothing can explain the mystical fact that two become one, we are not therefore entitled to assume that mystics, who have immediate experience of the fact, are pantheists in disguise. They may of course deserve that epithet, and if they themselves convert a state of feeling into a system of thought, they must bear the consequences.

Ibnu 'l-Fáriḍ, for the most part, simply relates the psychological history of his own experience. At the same time he teaches certain doctrines for which he claims the authority of the Koran and the Sunna. Among these is the doctrine—he gives it the name of *labs* (covering)—that the One God clothes Himself in the created forms through which He is revealed, as, for example, Gabriel is said to have appeared to the Prophet in the form of Diḥya al-Kalbí, one of the Prophet's Companions; but he warns the reader that this is something quite different from the heretical doctrine of incarnation (*ḥulúl*)[1]. Evidently he regarded himself as a Moslem, and the accounts of his life show that he was so regarded by most of his orthodox contemporaries. While in virtue of his union with God, or with the Prophetic Logos through whom

[1] *Tá'iyyatu 'l-Kubrá*, vv. 277–285.

God is manifested, he rose beyond all relations of time and space, beyond all the antinomies of human thought, he found the highest expression of that mystical unity within the religion of Islam As he tells us, he not only performed the rites of worship incumbent on every Moslem but added thereto the voluntary works of devotion by which the Ṣúfís seek to draw nigh unto God[1]. And it is no less significant that he concludes his poem with an emphatic assertion of the Moslem creed. All depends on the Will and Power of Allah. Allah misguides whomso He pleaseth and leads aright whomso He pleaseth (Kor. XVI, 95). Moslems, Christians, Jews, and Zoroastrians are what they are because Allah has decreed that so it shall be[2]. Here the poet cites the Tradition that when Allah created Adam, He drew forth his posterity from his loins in two handfuls, one white as silver and one black as coal, and said, "These are in Paradise and I care not; and these are in Hell and I care not[3]." Those of you who have read Professor Macdonald's admirable book, *The religious attitude and life in Islam*, may remember that he translates a passage in which the same Tradition is expounded by Ghazálí and makes the following comment:

> This is the end of the whole matter, and to this must return the vision of the Muslim mystic and the ecstasy of the Muslim saint; the dreams of a lover and beloved, and the groanings and travailings of creation. Whenever the devout life, with its spiritual aspirations and fervent longings, touches the scheme of Muslim theology, it must thus bend and break. For it, within Islam itself, there is no place[4].

Rather, I should say, there cannot logically be a place. For many Moslems are, in fact, Ṣúfís; and in Ṣúfism the

[1] *Tá'iyyatu 'l-Kubrá*, *vv*. 268–276 and *v*. 720.
[2] *Ibid*. *vv*. 733–741.
[3] *Ibid*. *v*. 746.
[4] *Op. cit.* p. 301.

God of Islam itself, the God who does not care, represents the aspect of extreme transcendence which, as we have seen, is often united with a consciousness of extreme immanence. This contrast is to some extent characteristic of the deepest religious feeling everywhere. For example, the Christian mystic commonly "identifies the personal and intimate Lover of the soul...with the person of Christ; the unknowable and transcendent Godhead with ...the Undifferentiated One in Whom the Trinity of Persons is resumed[1]." What Christianity conceives as the distinction of Persons in a Trinity is conceived by Islam as the distinction of aspects in a Unity. Allah as depicted in the Koran is mainly transcendent but is also immanent; the God of Ṣúfism is mainly immanent but is also transcendent. Only the Moslem scholastics, who make God absolutely transcendent, are thorough-going in their logic, though it must be allowed that some Ṣúfí pantheists have produced theories of immanence not unworthy to be set beside the orthodox theology.

It is hard to see how personal relations of love and worship can continue to exist in such a state of unification as Ibnu 'l-Fárid describes, especially as he himself declares that the supreme experience is beyond love[2]. Yet when he speaks, not of losing his permanent unitive state or of going outside of it, but of descending from his exaltation to perform ritual and devotional acts of worship, this can only mean that such acts, implying a personal relation to God, are consistent with his inner feeling and expressive of its true character.

I have tried to show you how close and vital is the connexion of Ṣúfism with the Mohammedan doctrine of Divine Unity, which affirms that God is transcendent,

[1] E. Underhill, *Mysticism*, p. 411.

[2] *Tá'iyya*, v. 294.

and how the Ṣúfís seek to realise that Unity and Transcendence by means of ecstasy, by passing away from themselves in order that God may make Himself known to them. And as Eckhart said, "All the truth which any master ever taught with his own reason and understanding, or ever can teach to the last day, will not in the least explain this knowledge[1]." For the truth about God can be declared by none but God—He alone has the right to say "I"[2]; and any man who may venture to give his testimony can only do so in virtue of having been purified and unified by God, made one with God, so that he actually represents in his own person the God whose truth he proclaims. In the first decade of the fourth century after Mohammed there came forward such a witness in the person of Ḥusayn ibn Manṣúr al-Ḥalláj, a native of Baydá in Fárs, the same town which produced the commentator Baydáwí Halláj, as you know, uttered the words *Ana 'l-Ḥaqq*, "I am God," and was executed at Baghdád in 309 A H. Perhaps you will hardly expect me to add that amongst the Mohammedan mystics, so far as I am acquainted with their writings, there is none whose doctrine is so original and whose religious experience cuts more deeply into life. Some facts bearing on this will be given in the next Lecture.

[1] Quoted by Rufus M Jones, *Studies in mystical religion*, p 232

[2] *Kitáb al-Luma'*, 32, 1

LECTURE II

MORE than fifty years ago Alfred von Kremer characterised the end of the third century after Mohammed as the epoch at which (to quote his own words)

"Moslem asceticism passed over into the pantheistic religious enthusiasm that forms the real essence of later Ṣúfism. Henceforth," he adds, "the notion of God, the conception of the reciprocal relations existing between the finite, the human, and the Infinite, the Divine, became the principal subject of investigation and reflection. The man who first gave precise expression to those ideas which till then had remained unknown to Arabian Ṣúfism inasmuch as they belonged to a quite different sphere of culture, was a poor artisan, a woolcarder by trade, for which reason he got the surname of Ḥalláj ... His life-story is variously recounted by Sunnite and Shí'ite authors, but this much stands fast, that he had a great number of followers who revered him as their teacher and guide and ascribed to him supernatural powers; that the orthodox party, alarmed by his ever increasing popularity, urged the Government to take measures against him; and that finally in the year 309 A.H. he was put to death, after having borne with amazing fortitude the frightful tortures inflicted on him."

I need not stop to discuss Von Kremer's view of the early history of Ṣúfism. As a matter of fact the ideas which he describes as foreign were an outgrowth of the ascetic and mystical movement in Islam and are mainly Islamic, though at some points Hellenistic influences may have cooperated, *e.g.* in the doctrine of gnosis (*ma'rifat*) taught by the Egyptian Ṣúfí, Dhu 'l-Nún († A.D. 859). On the other hand, the most eminent of Dhu 'l-Nún's contemporaries, Báyazíd, was a Persian; and during this period

1 *Gesch d. herrschenden Ideen des Islams*, p 70.

the influence of Persian thought (especially, perhaps, the doctrine of the Shí'ites who looked upon their Imáms as the personal representatives of God) had a large share in moulding these speculations, which gradually absorbed other elements of diverse origin. As regards the pantheistic character attributed by Von Kremer to the Súfism of which he takes Ḥalláj as the prototype, I hope to convince you that such a description is not applicable either to Halláj himself or to Ṣúfism in general. The development of Ṣúfí pantheism comes much later than Ḥalláj and was chiefly due to Ibnu 'l-'Arabí (A.D. 1165–1240). It would be a mistake to suppose that utterances like the *Subḥání*, "Glory to me," of Báyazíd, the *Ana 'l-Ḥaqq*, "I am God," of Ḥalláj, and the *Ana Hiya*, "I am She," of Ibnu 'l-Fáriḍ are in themselves evidence of pantheism. So long as transcendence is recognised, the most emphatic assertion of immanence is not pantheism but panentheism—not the doctrine that all is God, but the doctrine that all is *in* God, who is also above all. Moreover, excesses of mystical feeling must not be identified with theological beliefs. As a rule, Moslems have taken the view that between the saint and God there exists a mysterious relation which has to be respected even if it brings him into conflict with the religious law; but in the time of Ḥalláj the veneration of holy men had not yet gone so far as to put them out of danger. When Ḥalláj was brought to trial, the legal members of the court insisted that he should be impeached for having included the Pilgrimage to Mecca amongst the class of religious obligations that are not absolutely binding but admit of abrogation. This doctrine, together with the charge that he was in secret correspondence with the Carmathians, who nine years afterwards sacked Mecca and carried off the Black Stone, may have cost him his life. The fact that he declared himself to be essentially united with God was only one of the four heads under which he was arraigned, and by itself it might not have secured his condemnation, though, as we shall see, his teaching on this point took a form that rendered it peculiarly abominable to Moslems[1].

The words *Ana 'l-Ḥaqq* occur in an extraordinary book composed by Ḥalláj, the *Kitáb al-Ṭawásín*, which was edited in 1913 by M. Louis Massignon Written in rhymed Arabic prose and divided into eleven brief sections, it sets forth a doctrine of saintship—a doctrine founded on personal experience and clothed in the form of a subtle yet passionate dialectic. The style is so technical and obscure that even with the help of the Persian commentary we can sometimes only guess what meaning the writer intended to convey. Instead of translating the text[2], the editor has devoted years of patient labour to understanding and illustrating it, with the result that his monograph on Ḥalláj must be studied carefully by every one interested in Ṣúfism. For it is now clear that the words *Ana 'l-Ḥaqq* were not an ejaculation of visionary enthusiasm but the intuitive formula in which a whole system of mystical theology summed itself up. And this system is not only the first in time, it is also profoundly original. The power and vitality of this man's ideas are attested by the influence which they exerted upon his successors. His ash were scattered, swept away, as he prophesied, by rushing winds and running waters, but his words lived after him and we see them, all through the Middle Ages, rising like sparks and kindling to new life.

[1] An account of the trial, condemnation, and execution of Ḥalláj is given by Miskawaihi, ed Amedroz and Margoliouth, vol. I, pp. 76–82.

[2] It is translated in his *Passion* (see p. 37, note), vol. II, pp. 830–893.

I cannot attempt to give you a full account of the doctrines contained in the *Ṭawásín* and supplemented by numerous fragments which Massignon has collected. We may begin by asking, "What did Ḥalláj mean when he said *Ana 'l-Ḥaqq?*" The expression *al-Ḥaqq* is commonly used by Ṣúfís to denote the Creator as opposed to *al-khalq*, "the creatures," and there is no doubt that it bears this signification here: *Ana 'l-Ḥaqq*. "I am the Creative Truth," as Massignon renders it[1].

"Ḥalláj," he says, "while affirming the transcendence of the idea of God, did not at all conceive it as being inaccessible to man. From the old Jewish and Christian tradition that God created man in His own image Ḥalláj deduced a doctrine of creation, which had its counterpart in a doctrine of deification: the deified man finds in himself, by means of (a mystical) asceticism, the reality of the Divine image which God has imprinted on him. We possess several Ḥallájian fragments that leave no doubt as to this In the longest, Ḥalláj explains the matter thus: Before all things, before the creation, before His knowledge of the creation, God in His unity was holding an ineffable discourse with Himself and contemplating the splendour of His essence in itself That pure simplicity of His self-admiration is Love, which in His essence is the essence of the essence, beyond all limitation of attributes In His perfect isolation God loves Himself, praises Himself, and manifests Himself by Love. And it was this first manifestation of Love in the Divine Absolute that determined the multiplicity of His attributes and His names. Then God, by His essence, in His essence, desired to project out of Himself His supreme joy, that Love in aloneness, that He might behold it and speak to it He looked in eternity and brought forth from non-existence an image, an image of Himself, endowed with all His attributes and all His names: Adam. The Divine look made that form to be His image unto everlasting. God saluted it, glorified it, chose it, and inasmuch as He manifested Himself by it and in it, that created form became *Huwa Huwa*, He, He[2]"

[1] *Kitáb al-Ṭawásín*, p. 175.

[2] *Ibid* p 129 fol.

The first of the following verses by Ḥalláj refers to Adam, the second is said to refer to Jesus:

Glory to God who revealed in His humanity the secret of His radiant divinity,
And then appeared to His creatures visibly in the shape of one who eats and drinks[1].

Here, you will notice, we have the doctrine of two natures in God—a divine nature (*láhút*) and a human nature (*násút*). These terms are borrowed from Syrian Christianity, which uses them to denote the two natures of Christ. Further, Halláj in describing the union of the *láhút* with the *násút*—or, as he generally says, of the Divine Spirit with the human spirit—employs the term *ḥulúl*; and *ḥulúl* is a word associated, in Moslem minds, with the Christian doctrine of the Incarnation. In his poems his own spirit and the Divine Spirit appear as lovers conversing with each other and most intimately united.

Thy Spirit is mingled in my spirit even as wine is mingled with pure water.
When anything touches Thee, it touches me. Lo, in every case Thou art I[2].

And again:

I am He whom I love, and He whom I love is I,
We are two spirits dwelling in one body.
If thou seest me, thou seest Him,
And if thou seest Him, thou seest us both[3].

While Ḥalláj asserts the pre-existence of Mohammed as the Light from which all prophecy emanates[4], it is not Mohammed but Jesus in whom he finds the perfect type of the "deified man," whose personality is not destroyed

[1] *Kitáb al-Ṭawásín*, p. 130.
[2] *Ibid.* p. 134
[3] *Ibid.* p. 134.
[4] *Ibid.* p 11

but transfigured and essentialised, so that he stands forth as the personal witness and representative of God, revealing from within himself *al-Ḥaqq*, the Creator through whom he exists, the Creative Truth in whom he has all his being[1]. You will agree that this is singular doctrine on the lips of a Mohammedan. It is entirely opposed to pantheism, for it makes the human nature an image of the Divine, though not quite in the same sense that caused Christ to say, "He that hath seen me hath seen the Father[2]." A doctrine which is described, even metaphorically, as *ḥulúl* could not take root in Islam. It perished with Ḥalláj and his immediate disciples. The majority of the later Ṣúfís extol him as a martyr who died on the scaffold because he dared to reveal the Divine mystery, but they deny that he taught *ḥulúl* and interpret his *Ana 'l-Ḥaqq* in a Unitarian or monistic sense, thus giving it a flavour of orthodoxy but altogether disguising the features which make it so remarkable. Hence in the development of his ideas by Ibnu 'l-'Arabí and Jílí the living clash of personality, Divine and human, resolves itself into a logical distinction between God and man as aspects of the One Essence, whose attributes receive their most perfect manifestation in the first-created Light of Mohammed, the Prophet of Allah.

Strange as it may seem, Ḥalláj, who found his model of the saintly life in Jesus Christ, celebrates as exponents of the true mystical doctrine of Divine Unity not only Pharaoh but especially Iblís, the Mohammedan Diabolus. The Koran, as you will remember, tells in several places how God commanded the angels to worship Adam, and how Iblís—his name was then 'Azázíl—refused, saying, "I am more excellent than he: Thou hast created me of

[1] *Kitáb al-Ṭawásín*, pp. 161, 175. [2] John XIV, 9.

fire and him of clay[1]"; whereupon God cursed him and cast him into Hell. From the Unitarian point of view, to worship Adam, even though Adam be regarded as the Divine image, is idolatry, and Ḥalláj was not the first Devil's advocate in Islam. According to him if Iblís disobeyed the Divine command, it was only because he would not acknowledge any object of worship except the One God. When God threatened him with everlasting punishment, Iblís asked, "Wilt not Thou behold me whilst Thou art punishing me?" God answered, "Yes." "Then," said Iblís, "Thy beholding me will take away from me consciousness of the punishment. Do unto me as Thou wilt![2]" And in another dialogue Iblís, being reproached by Moses for his disobedience, replies, "It was not a command, it was a trial"—meaning a test of his devotion to God[3]. So Ḥalláj can make Iblís say, "In refusing to obey Thee I glorified Thee[4]" (*juḥúdí laka taqdís*), and can declare that Iblís and Pharaoh are his "friends and teachers."

"If ye do not recognise God," he says, "at least recognise His signs. I am that sign, I am the Creative Truth (*Ana 'l-Ḥaqq*), because through the Truth I am a truth eternally. My friends and teachers are Iblís and Pharaoh. Iblís was threatened with Hell-fire, yet he did not recant. Pharaoh was drowned in the sea, yet he did not recant, for he would not acknowledge anything between him and God. And I, though I am killed and crucified, and though my hands and feet are cut off—I do not recant![5]"

But Ḥalláj, be it observed, while praising the self-sacrifice (*futuwwat*) shown by Iblís in upholding the Divine Unity, condemns him for disobeying the Divine command. Iblís justified his disobedience by the plea

[1] Kor. VII, 11 [2] *Kitáb al-Ṭawásín*, p. xii.
[3] *Ibid.* p. 46. [4] *Ibid.* p. 43. [5] *Ibid.* pp. 51–52.

that he knew it to be predestined. God *commanded* him to worship Adam, but *willed* that he should refuse; otherwise he must have obeyed, since God *wills* nothing that does not come to pass. Ḥalláj, on the other hand, insists that obedience is a sacred duty. The *command* (*amr*) is eternal, whereas the *will* (*mashiyyat*) and foreknowledge of God concerning it, whether it shall be obeyed or disobeyed, is created, and therefore subordinate. God *wills* both good and evil, but *commands* only good. He *commands* us to do a thing and foreknows that we cannot do it, He *wills* that we sin, but He does not will that we sin by our own fault[1]. Ḥalláj, as Massignon says, realised profoundly the bitterness of the dilemma, which he states in a verse quoted by Ibn Khallikán:

> God cast him into the sea, with his arms tied behind his back,
> And said to him, "Take care, take care, lest thou be wetted by the water![2]"

That might be the final word from Iblís, who, pretending to have read the secret of Divine Providence, gave way to despair. Halláj, however, knew that the essence of God is Love, and that it is the essence of Love to suffer without asking for reasons. It behoves the true saint to turn towards God in humble adoration and strive with all his heart to fulfil the Divine command, no matter at what cost of suffering to himself. Such, apparently, was the gist of the religious teaching of Ḥalláj, so far as we may judge from the testimonies preserved by his disciples. Let me quote one or two of these

Ibráhím ibn Fátik relates as follows: When Ḥusayn ibn Manṣúr al-Ḥalláj was brought to be crucified, and saw the cross and the nails, he laughed so greatly and

[1] *Kitáb al-Ṭawásín*, pp 145–148

[2] *Wafayát al-A'yán*, ed De Slane, p 21,

violently that tears flowed from his eyes. Then he turned to the people and seeing Shiblí among them said to him, "O Abú Bakr, hast thou thy prayer-carpet with thee?" Shiblí answered, "Yes, O Shaykh!" Ḥalláj bade him spread it out, which he did. Then Ḥalláj stepped forward and prayed two *rak'as* on it, and I was near to him. In the first *rak'a* he recited the *Fátiḥa* and a verse of the Koran, namely,

Every soul shall taste of death. Ye shall be given your full rewards on the day of Resurrection, and whoso shall be put far from Hell-fire and caused to enter Paradise, happy is he! The present life is but the goods of vanity[1].

In the second *rak'a* he recited the *Fátiḥa* and a verse of the Koran, namely,

We will surely try thee with somewhat of fear and hunger and loss of wealth and lives and fruits. And bring a message of joy unto the patient who say, when an affliction befalls them, "Lo, we belong to God and to Him we shall return." Those are they upon whom are blessings from their Lord and mercy, and those are in the right way[2].

And when he had finished, he uttered a prayer of which I remember only these words:

...O Lord, I beseech Thee to make me thankful for the grace Thou hast bestowed upon me in concealing from the eyes of other men what Thou hast revealed to me of the splendours of Thy radiant countenance which is without a form, and in making it lawful for me to behold the mysteries of Thy inmost conscience which Thou hast made unlawful to other men. And these Thy servants who are gathered to slay me, in zeal for Thy religion and in desire to win Thy favour, pardon them and have mercy upon them; for verily if Thou hadst revealed to them that which Thou hast revealed to me, they would not have done what they have done; and if Thou hadst hidden from me that which Thou

[1] Kor. III, 182. [2] Kor. II, 150–152.

hast hidden from them, I should not have suffered this tribulation. Glory unto Thee in whatsoever Thou doest, and glory unto Thee in whatsoever Thou willest!

Then he remained silent for a time, communing with his Lord, until Abu 'l-Ḥárith, the executioner, went and smote him on the cheek, breaking his nose with the blow, so that the blood gushed out. Thereat Shiblí cried aloud and rent his garment and fell in a swoon, and so did Abu 'l-Ḥusayn al-Wásiṭí and a number of well-known Ṣúfís. And it almost came to a riot[1]

On another occasion the same disciple visited Ḥalláj in his house.

He said, "Come in! be not afraid," so I came in and seated myself before him, and lo, his eyes were as two sparks of fire and bloodshot. "O my son," said he, "some bear witness for me, saying that I am a saint, and others bear witness against me, saying that I am an unbeliever. They that bear witness that I am an unbeliever are dearer to me and to God than those who bear witness that I am a saint" I said, "And why is that, O Shaykh?" "Because," he replied, "they that bear witness to my saintship do so on account of their good thoughts concerning me, while those who bear witness to my unbelief do so from zeal for their religion; and whosoever is zealous for his religion is dearer to me and dearer to God than one who thinks well of any man" Then he said to me, "And how will it be with thee, O Ibráhím, when thou seest me crucified and killed and burnt, and that day the happiest of all the days of my life?" Then he said to me, "Do not sit here. Go forth, and God protect thee![2]"

One day Ḥalláj entered the mosque of Manṣúr at Baghdád and said, "O people, come together and hear news from me." A great multitude gathered to him, so many that only God could number them. Some of them

[1] Massignon, *Quatre textes inédites, relatifs à la biographie d'al-Hosayn ibn Manṣoûr al-Ḥallâj* (1914), p. 51*.

[2] *Ibid.* p. 54*.

loved Ḥallāj and believed in him, others hated and denied him. "Ye must know," said he, "that God hath made my blood lawful unto you, therefore kill me!" The people wept, and 'Abd al-Wadúd ibn Sa'íd ibn 'Abd al-Ghaní, the ascetic, came forward and asked,

> O Shaykh, how should we kill a man who performs the canonical prayers and keeps the fast and recites the Koran?

Ḥallāj answered him and said,

> O Shaykh, the cause for which it is forbidden to shed a man's blood lies not in the canonical prayer and the fast and the reciting of the Koran. Kill me, that ye may be rewarded and that I may have rest, so shall ye be fighters for the Faith and I a martyr[1].

In Mohammedan mysticism it is prayer that supplies the best evidence of personality—not the ritual prayer (*ṣalát*), but the free prayer (*du'á*) and in particular the loving converse with God (*munáját*), when the mystic speaks out of the depths of his heart. One specimen of the *munáját* of Ḥallāj has been quoted already. Here is another.

> O God, because of what I feel of the sweet breaths of Thy love and the perfume of Thy presence I despise the solid mountains and hold the earths and the heavens in contempt. By Thy truth, if Thou wouldst sell me Paradise in exchange for a single moment of my ecstasy or for one passing gleam of the least of my spiritual states, I would not buy it! And if Thou wert to set Hell-fire before me, with all the diverse kinds of torment that are contained therein, I would deem it of no account in comparison with my suffering when Thou hidest Thyself from me. Forgive the people and do not forgive me, and have mercy on them and do not have mercy on me! I do not plead with Thee for my own sake, nor do I implore Thee in my own right. Do unto me as Thou wilt![2]

The legend of a saint gives us impressions of his personality rather than facts, and whatever the historical

[1] Massignon, *Quatre textes*, p. 63*. [2] *Ibid.* p. 78*.

value of these documents may be, they show at any rate how the life and religious experience of Ḥalláj was regarded by those nearest to him. It is a striking picture and I believe it is essentially a true one. You will have noticed that some of its features might have been drawn from a Christian original—I mean, of course, the prominence given to the virtues of charity, meekness and humility, and above all to the idea of holiness made perfect by suffering. It is possible to hold that Ḥalláj taught a doctrine of incarnation, and his prayer, "Forgive the people and do not forgive me: I do not plead with Thee for my own sake," appears to suggest a doctrine of vicarious sacrifice. That he was no pantheist will now be clear to you. Like all the Ṣúfís of his age, he affirms both transcendence and immanence, and it is a mark of his intense personality that while his *Ana 'l-Ḥaqq* unites the two extremes he finds the truest champion of the former in Iblís and the most complete type of the latter in Jesus. In taking leave of Ḥalláj I must again express my obligation to M. Massignon for his labour in collecting the materials used in the present sketch as well as for the wide learning and sympathetic insight with which he has interpreted them[1].

A personality of very different order is Abú Ḥámid Ghazálí. Moslems have often said that if there could have been a prophet after Mohammed, Ghazálí would have been the man. Although his career as a whole lies beyond the scope of these Lectures and in fact belongs to Islam rather than to Ṣúfism, it was as a Ṣúfí that he had the illuminating experiences which inspired all his work and

[1] His monumental work in two volumes, *La Passion d'al-Hosayn ibn Mansour al-Hallaj* (Paris, 1922) appeared too late for me to make use of it.

in virtue of which his name is linked with the revival of personal religion in Islam. You are familiar with the course of his life, at least in outline—how, for all his theological training, he was a born critic, so that "in his earliest youth he had given up acceptance of religious truth on authority"; how he sought to discover a real basis for knowledge and, finding none, drifted into utter scepticism; how he passed through a crisis in which "the light of God" entered his heart; how he then regained the power to think, and setting forth in search of the truth turned at last to the writings of the Ṣúfís and saw that he was now on the right track; how, though he felt himself to be in a false position—for he held a Professorship of Divinity at Baghdád—he could not make up his mind to abandon the world until under the strain of this moral conflict his health broke down and in despair he took refuge with God, who made the sacrifice easy to him; how he left Baghdád and lived in retirement for ten years, during which time he learned Ṣúfism not from books but from actual experience; and how, after having resumed his public teaching for a short while, he went back to his birthplace, Ṭús in Khurásán, where he died in A.D. 1111.

All this is related by Ghazálí himself in his book entitled "The Deliverer from Error" (*al-Munqidh min al-ḍalál*), of which the autobiographical part runs almost exactly parallel with the experience of St Augustine as recorded in the *Confessions*. Ghazálí, like St Augustine, distinguishes two stages in the process by which he attained to the truth. The first stage, the Divine illumination whereby he was led out of the wilderness of scepticism, he dismisses in a few words.

"God healed me," he says, "of this malady, and my soul regained its health and balance. Once more I accepted the first principles of thought with confidence in their certainty and security. This was not the result of logical proofs but was effected by means of a light which God threw into my heart; and that light is the key to most kinds of knowledge[1]."

Here he quotes a Tradition of the Prophet, who, on being asked to explain the meaning of the text "God will open his breast to Islam" (Kor. VI, 125), replied, "'Tis a light which God throws into the heart, and the sign thereof is a drawing back from the world of vanity and a turning towards the world everlasting." The last words indicate the road which Ghazálí was to take, but the second stage of his conversion was separated from the first by a long interval of time. He could now walk by the light of faith—not unquestioning faith, however. He was still a seeker, uncertain what path would lead him to the goal. Amongst his contemporaries there were four classes of men whose claims he had to examine, namely, the scholastic theologians, the philosophers, the Ta'límís or believers in an infallible Imám, and the Ṣúfís. His investigation and refutation of scholasticism, philosophy, and what may be called Mohammedan popery, occupies a dozen pages of the *Munqidh*. He then comes to the climax, which I must give as it stands in the original, though with some abridgement.

"Then," he says, "I turned my attention to the Way of the Ṣúfís. I knew that it could not be traversed to the end without both doctrine and practice, and that the gist of their doctrine lies in overcoming the appetites of the flesh and getting rid of its evil dispositions and vile qualities, so that the heart may be cleared of all but God; and the means of clearing it is *dhikr Allah, i.e.* commemoration of God and concentration of every thought upon Him. Now, the doctrine was easier to me than the practice, so I began by learning their doctrine from the books and sayings of their Shaykhs, until I acquired as much of their Way as it is possible to

[1] *Munqidh* (Cairo, 1309 A.H.), p. 5.

acquire by learning and hearing, and saw plainly that what is most peculiar to them cannot be learned, but can only be reached by immediate experience and ecstasy and inward transformation. How great is the difference between knowing the definition, causes, and conditions of drunkenness and actually being drunk! The drunken man knows nothing about the definition and theory of drunkenness, but he is drunk; while the sober man, knowing the definition and the principles of drunkenness, is not drunk at all I became convinced that the Ṣúfís are men of feeling (*arbábu aḥwál*), not men of words (*aṣḥábu aqwál*), and that I had now acquired all the knowledge of Ṣúfism that could possibly be obtained by means of study; as for the rest, there was no way of coming to it except by leading the mystical life From my examination of the religious and intellectual sciences I had gained a sure faith in God, in prophecy, and in the last Judgment These three cardinal points of faith were fixed in my heart. It had also become clear to me that my hope of happiness in the next world depended on fearing God and mortifying the flesh, and that in the first place I must detach myself from all worldly ties and turn wholly to God. I looked on myself as I then was Worldly interests encompassed me on every side. Even my work as a teacher—the best thing I was engaged in—seemed unimportant and useless in view of the life hereafter. When I considered the intention of my teaching, I perceived that instead of doing it for God's sake alone I had no motive but the desire for glory and reputation. I realised that I stood on the edge of a precipice and would fall into Hell fire unless I set about to mend my ways[1]."

Ghazálí describes in vivid language the ensuing struggle with himself which lasted for six months. One day he would make a firm resolution to sacrifice everything and leave Baghdád, only to break it on the morrow. He heard the voice of faith calling him to depart, while as often as he moved a foot forward the lusts of this world dragged him back Torn asunder by two forces contending for mastery, he lost the power of speech, and after making

[1] *Munqidh*, pp. 20–21.

a vain effort to lecture was stricken with melancholia He could no longer digest his food. The physicians gave him up. Then at last he gave himself up.

"Conscious of my helplessness and having surrendered my will entirely, I took refuge with God as a man in sore trouble who has no resource left God answered my prayer and made it easy for me to turn my back on reputation and wealth and wife and children and friends[1]"

So he quitted Baghdád, with the resolve never to enter it again. His age at this time was thirty-seven. He went to Syria, where he passed two years in seclusion, practising the ascetic and religious discipline of the Ṣúfís; and until he died, twenty-three years after his flight from Baghdád, his life to a large extent was that of a mystic.

Ghazálí's account of his mystical experience leaves no doubt that he owed to this experience, and to this alone, the real knowledge that was the object of his search. But while his religious and ethical teaching has its roots in Ṣúfism, and while his writings are saturated with Ṣúfistic ideas, he himself was more than a Ṣúfí, otherwise he could not have done the work he did. He used the methods of critical philosophy to show that religion is the birthright of man as such, that all the powers and activities peculiar to man point to a faculty which is not of this world and which enables its possessor to move in the world of reality, and that even the highest religious experience—that of the prophets and saints—though it passes human understanding, is none the less grounded in human nature. All this indeed is contained in the favourite Ṣúfí texts—"God created Adam in His own image," and "He who knows himself knows his Lord"; but Ghazálí, instead of regarding it as a mystery reserved for the elect, starts from a broad psychological basis and treats the subject

[1] *Munqidh* p. 21, at foot.

in a way that appeals to the minds and consciences of all who seek the truth. Here lies his strength and also, perhaps, his weakness. The personal note is almost lacking, or rather, his personality hardly ever expresses itself in the form given by direct religious experience. The autobiographical passages of the *Munqidh* stand alone. Concerning his inner life after he left Baghdád he tells us nothing. The curtain drops, and we have to content ourselves with the information that ineffable things were revealed to him, and with a brief description of the stages whereby Ṣúfís attain to the unitive state. An interesting comparison and contrast of Ghazálí with Augustine has recently appeared, in which the author, a young German scholar, declares that whereas the personality of Augustine was made complete through the living relation of his soul to God and to the person of Christ, the spiritual development of Ghazálí culminates in his acknowledgment of the truth of prophecy and his consequent submission to the authority of the church. According to this view,

even when Ghazálí speaks with admiration of the moral virtues of the Prophet, he does not get beyond the thought of an infallible doctrine, a revelation whose truth stands fast, a knowledge which is to be secured from criticism and stamped with divine authority by invoking the moral preeminence of him who promulgated it. Thus here also, where Augustine displays the deepest inwardness of his feeling, Ghazálí is seen still clinging to intellectualism. True, he made a push forward into the region of super-intellectual experience, but he had not power enough for personality to break right through, and he always came back upon the single line of his whole development, to the problem of gaining unshakable knowledge of Truth. That was in a sense the tragic thing in his life[1].

[1] H. Frick, *Ghazālīs Selbstbiographie ein Vergleich mit Augustins Konfessionen* (Leipzig, 1919), p. 80.

It is obvious that we cannot discuss Christian or Mohammedan ideas of personality without reference to the persons of Christ and Mohammed, since the archetype, whether it be historical or ideal, necessarily determines the nature of every imitation of it. The Christian idea of personality, that is, of personal relationship to God, is the Christian idea of Christ, and the Mohammedan idea of personality is the Mohammedan idea of Mohammed. Of course, neither of these ideas represents an absolutely fixed standard; both are subject to variation and development. Far apart at first, they moved nearer to each other as time went on. My next Lecture will show that the Prophet of medieval Islam was invested with some of the attributes of the Christ worshipped by St John and St Paul; and it looks as though the trend of modern thought in the West would invert that process and leave Christ with as little divinity as Mohammed claimed for himself.

The problem of Ghazálí's relation to the Prophet is beset with difficulties. That he was fully conscious of its importance appears from the *Munqidh*, where the account of his final conversion is immediately followed by a chapter on the truth of prophecy." The truth of prophecy: this was the answer to the question which he had asked himself in the days of his intellectual scepticism—"What is Truth?" In order to find that answer, he had to become a mystic, he had to pass through a personal religious experience which convinced him that rationalists who deny prophecy are like men born blind. Let me quote what he says of the Ṣúfís:

> All their outward actions and inward states are irradiated by the light of the lamp of prophecy, and there is not on the face of the earth any other light from which illumination

should be sought.... Unless a man has felt in himself some part of this matter (*i.e.* of the highest mystical states), he knows nothing of prophecy, as it really is, except the name. The miraculous gifts of the Ṣúfí saints are the first things that happen to the prophets (*i.e.* the prophets begin with experiences similar to those of the Ṣúfís) Such was the case with Mohammed at the outset, when he retired to Mt Ḥirá to be alone with God and gave himself up to devotion[1].

Ghazálí goes on to say that the truth of prophecy may be learned indirectly by considering the phenomena of dreams, by studying the Koran and the Ḥadíth, and by other methods which he explains, but the passage translated above brings out the essential fact that he himself gained assurance of the truth of prophecy by experiencing something analogous to that which constitutes the very nature of a prophet. This would seem to imply a personal relation in which Mohammed is not only the supreme religious and moral authority but the source and inspiration of moral and religious life.

In this connexion I may refer to Ghazálí's esoteric doctrine. He often hints at mysteries which he could reveal if it were wise and safe to speak plainly. Thus in one of his latest books, the *Mishkát al-Anwár*, he introduces a Being to whom he gives the name of *al-Muṭá'*, "the Obeyed One[2]." The *Muṭá'* is Allah's Khalífa or Vicegerent, the supreme controller of the whole Universe, and the relation of Allah to him is likened to "the relation of the impalpable light-essence to the sun, or of the elemental fire to a glowing coal." Now, it is clear that in the conception of the *Muṭá'* we have before us a Mo-

[1] *Munqidh*, p. 23.

[2] See W. H. T. Gairdner, "Al-Ghazālī's Mishkāt al-Anwār and the Ghazālī-Problem," in *Der Islam* (1914), pp. 121–153.

hammedan Logos doctrine. That being so, the term *Muṭá'* inevitably suggests the Koranic *amr*, the Divine "Command," through which God works His will on the world, and from which the prophets receive their inspiration[1]. Is the *Muṭá'* a personification of the *amr*? [2] That explanation would fit in very well with Ghazálí's psychology.

"It is recorded in tradition," writes Macdonald, "that the Prophet said, 'God Most High created Adam in His own form (*súra*).' Al-Ghazzálí takes that to mean that there is a likeness between the spirit of man and God in essence, quality, and actions. Further, the spirit of man rules the body as God rules the world. Man's body is a microcosm beside the macrocosm of this world, and they correspond, part by part Is, then, God simply the *anima mundi*? No, because He is the creator of all by His will, the sustainer and destroyer by His will. Al-Ghazzálí comes to this by a study of himself. His primary conception is *volo ergo sum*. It is not thought which impresses him, but volition. From thought he can develop nothing; from will can come the whole round universe[3]."

The *Mishkát* contradicts this passage in one particular. God indeed remains the creator of the world, but He is no longer in any direct sense its ruler. He is absolutely transcendent, and since the moving of the heavenly spheres would be incompatible with His unity, that function is assigned to "One by whose command the spheres are moved," *i.e.* to the *Muṭá'*. The *Muṭá'* is not identical with God: he must therefore be a created being. But who or what is he? It has been suggested that he may

[1] See H. Grimme, "Der Logos in Südarabien," in *Nöldeke-Festschrift*, I, 453 foll.

[2] Cf. Ibnu 'l-'Arabí, *Tadbírát*, ed. Nyberg, p. 122, ll. 1–11, and *ibid.*, *Einleitung*, pp. 106–108, where the Logos doctrine of Ghazálí is discussed.

[3] D. B. Macdonald, *Development of Muslim Theology*, pp. 231 fol.

be the Quṭb, the head of the Ṣúfí hierarchy, but this seems very unlikely when we consider that Ghazálí always rejected and opposed the Shí'ite = Ismá'ílí Imám-doctrine, from which the Ṣúfí Quṭb-doctrine was probably derived. I am rather disposed to think that in this matter Ghazálí was in accord with later mystical speculations, and that the *Muṭá'* represents the archetypal Spirit of Mohammed, the Heavenly Man created in the image of God[1] and regarded as a Cosmic Power on whom depends the order and preservation of the universe[2]. According to the Koran (XVII, 87), the spirit (*al-rúḥ*) belongs to the *amr* of God[3], and Jílí, a famous mystic of the fourteenth century, says that one of the names of the Divine Spirit, the Spirit of which Mohammed is the perfect manifestation, is *Amr Allah*, *i.e.* the "Command" of God, the Logos[4]. Ghazálí may have borrowed the name *Muṭá'* from a Koranic text (III, 29) of great importance for the Mohammedan Logos doctrine—"Say: if ye love Allah, follow me, so will Allah love you and forgive you your sins, for Allah is forgiving and merciful. Say: obey Allah and the Apostle (*atí'u 'lláha wa-r-rasúl*)." Those of you who read Arabic know that the word *Muṭá'* is the parti-

[1] Ghazálí often alludes mysteriously to this Ḥadíth. Cf Gairdner, *op. cit* p 152

[2] See Lecture III.

[3] Zamakhsharí (*Kashsháf*, ed. Nassau Lees, p 783) explains *amr* by *waḥy*, inspiration, and *kalám*, word He mentions three different interpretations of *al-rúḥ*: (1) a mighty spiritual creature, mightier than the angel; (2) Gabriel, (3) the Koran The first of these could be applied to the Spirit of Mohammed in the sense defined above, the last is obviously not Ghazálí's Logos; and the possibility of identifying the *Muṭá'* with Gabriel (who is described by the epithet *muṭá'* in Kor LXXXI, 21) appears to be excluded by Ghazálí's remark (Gairdner, *op cit* p 141) that "the rank of Seraphiel may well be above that of Gabriel." Moreover, the *Muṭá'* is nowhere called an angel

[4] *Studies in Islamic Mysticism*, p 110.

ciple of the same verb of which *aṭí'ú* is the imperative. The Divine order to obey Mohammed implies that, for every good Moslem, Mohammed is *al-Muṭá'*, "the Obeyed One."

If the above hypothesis be accepted, Ghazálí believed that while God in His essence is known only to those who have realised His unity in the all-consuming mystical experience, His will and providence are manifested in the world through the Idea embodied, as it were, in the person of Mohammed[1]. But exactly what such a belief may have meant for him, I am unable to say. In the *Munqidh* the Prophet is described as a physician skilled in the healing of souls, one who was more than a father to his people in his tender and loving care for their well-being[2]. I must admit that neither here nor elsewhere does Ghazálí use the language of personal intimacy. As a rule, to quote Canon Gairdner, "his thought is cast in the theological mould"; and though his books tell us much about the communion of the saints with God, a few pages contain the whole history of his own inner life so far as he attempts to reveal it. Perhaps the truth is that he lacked the power of immediate self-expression, so that where he writes from the heart his words strike the mind and stir the conscience before we recognise that they could not affect us so strongly unless they rose from a spring of feeling within—from what Tennyson has called "the abysmal deeps of Personality."

I would recommend students of Ghazálí to read a little

[1] The *Muṭá'* can scarcely be distinguished from the Koranic *amr* = *rúh* in any case. While there is no positive evidence that Ghazálí identified the latter with Mohammed, this would seem to be a natural development from his views as to the spiritual essence of Man and the divine origin of prophecy.

[2] *Munqidh*, p. 33.

book by Gerald Gould, first published four years ago and entitled, *The Helping Hand: an essay in philosophy and religion for the unhappy*. The author's religious experiences, his methods, and many of his ideas have an astonishing resemblance to those of the great Moslem seeker of God. Time does not allow me to draw out the parallel in detail, but I should like to quote without comment one or two passages which seem to me to illustrate the religious attitude of Ghazálí better than anything I have read. Their value is increased by the fact that, being neither theological nor mystical, they meet Ghazálí on the common human ground to which—and this is the real secret of his vitality—he always returns in his treatment of religious problems.

"If" says Mr Gould, "the ultimate answer to all questions is religion, then inevitably, as far as my book has any truth or worth at all, it will be a religious book.....My message is from one who has been a troubled seeker to others who are troubled and who seek. I have no qualification as a religious teacher except that which is ordinarily regarded as a disqualification—that I share the common evil and know the common bitterness I have wandered like so many thousands and millions of my fellows, in the darkness of scepticism which questioned not merely this creed or that, but every guide, standard and opinion in turn. If, as I cannot help believing, I have found a guide amid the darkness, and an assurance of final light, the guide and the assurance are such as any one else may find. Again and again I come back to the commonness of the experience, the universal possibility of hope....A good deal of what I shall say is necessarily old, though I hope to put it in a new light by means of new arrangement. I shall cover a good deal of ground that is familiar to the student of religious or philosophical problems. But, student of these problems as I have been myself for years, it is not as a student, or for students, that I write.... It is part of my deliberate purpose to avoid quotation of works which deal with religion and philosophy as controversial subjects. If I refer to some of the known facts or attractive theories embraced in academic metaphysics and psychology, it will be by way of reference to subordinate adjuncts of the main theme My main theme is an appeal from common experience to common experience. I want to bring home a great central truth, as it has been brought home to me[1] "

You may find nearly all this, either expressed or implied, in Ghazálí. Take, again, the topic of repentance. Ghazálí shows that repentance is a universal human experience, a necessary consequence of self-knowledge[2]. This is also the argument of Mr Gould:

> To repent is to recognise the singleness of the self (which implies responsibility for past action) and the duality of the self (which implies the freedom of the present self from the bondage of the past) ...The Christian is assured by his religion that he cannot be forgiven by God unless he takes the *practical* step of turning his back upon the sin: the agnostic does not feel easy in his mind, cannot conquer the sense of shame and degradation involved in the recognition of his own sinfulness, unless he takes the *practical* step of turning his back upon the sin[3]

Mr Gould's conclusion is quite in the spirit of Ghazálí:

> The teaching of religion on this point, in short, is as it were a *reading*, an interpretation in the light of certain beliefs, of a common human experience which not the least religious can escape. And it is, I think, infinitely important that the non-religious should realise this—should realise that religion does not present, as so often it is made to seem to do, a strange and alien face to everyday doings and feelings: does not depend for its consolations wholly upon remote and abstract conceptions which the plain man cannot hope to understand: does not embody itself in maxims which have a "supernatural" sanction only, so that if the "super-

[1] *Op. cit.* pp. 1–4.

[2] Cf J. Obermann, *Der philosophische und religiöse Subjektivismus Ghazālīs*, pp. 231 foll.

[3] *The Helping Hand*, pp 71–81

natural" does not mean anything to one's intelligence, the maxims cannot mean anything to one's heart. The opposite of all these mistakes is the simple truth. The Christian religion (and of many other religions this is also true, but we must here take the Christian as a type) fits closely in its teaching to the actual movements of the heart and mind[1].

Mr Gould asks, "What is the essence of the finality which we recognise in religion?" and answers, "It is *personality*. That is the distinguishing mark: that is the clue to our puzzles.... The test of religion is the personal and spiritual peace, the *assurance*, that it brings[2]." Mr Gould found this in Christ, Ghazálí found it in Mohammed—in the Prophet whom Allah loves, and who is loved and obeyed by all who love and obey Allah.

I had intended to make some remarks on Jalálu'ddín Rúmí, but they must be left over for our next meeting as the hour is late. In order that Ghazálí may have the last word, you will allow me to read the beautiful prayer with which he concludes the *Munqidh*:

> We pray Almighty God that He will set us amongst those whom He hath preferred and chosen, those whom He hath guided and led to the Truth, those whom He hath inspired to think on Him so that they forget Him not, those whom He hath preserved from the evil of the flesh so that they choose Him above all else, those whom He hath devoted to Himself so that they worship none but Him![3]

[1] *The Helping Hand*, pp. 81 fol. [2] *Ibid.* p. 93.
[3] *Munqidh*, p. 34.

LECTURE III

BEFORE pursuing the ideas suggested by the doctrine of a Khalífa or Vicegerent through whom the world is brought into personal relation with its Creator, I will ask you to turn for refreshment to a mystical poet whose personality finds utterance "in the language of emotion and imagination rather than in that of the intellect[1]." Jalálu'ddín Rúmí holds that intellect, as opposed to love, is of the Devil[2]; he scorns book-learning and traditional knowledge, and he must have condemned the scientific and philosophical method of Ghazálí as alien to the true spirit of Ṣúfism, while Ghazálí on his part would have viewed with grave reprobation the ecstatic flights which carry Jalálu'ddín far above the realms of morality and law. To a certain extent the teaching of the *Iḥyá* and the *Masnaví* is the same, but the teachers are very different. Ghazálí is systematic, precise, and lucid; Jalálu'ddín allegorical, rambling, tedious, often obscure; yet Ghazálí can seldom compete with him in ardour and exaltation of feeling, in originality and profundity of thought, or in power and freedom of expression. On the other hand Jalálu'ddín writes for Ṣúfís alone, whereas Ghazálí demonstrates that knowledge of God is not peculiar to any one class of mankind—not even to the prophets and saints, who possess it, as Jalálu'ddín says, *essentially*[3]—but concerns all and may

[1] Whinfield, *Masnaví*, 2nd ed. (1898), p. xxxv.
[2] *Zíraki z Iblís u 'ishq az Adam ast.*
[3] Whinfield, *Masnaví*, p. 155.

be acquired by all. Neither the theologian nor the poet is a pantheist. From Ghazálí we get the science and doctrine, from Jalálu'ddín the sentiment, faith, and experience of personal religion. I am aware that, as regards Jalálu'ddín, this judgment may appear questionable to those who have read certain passages in the *Díwáni Shamsi Tabríz* where he describes his oneness with God in terms which look pantheistic at first sight and which I myself understood in a pantheistic sense at a time when I knew less about the history of Ṣúfism than I do now. As we saw in the case of Ibnu 'l-Fáriḍ, the mystic who has attained to the unitive state can identify himself with the all-comprehending reality of God. Jalálu'ddín, for example, says in one of his odes:

> I am the theft of rogues, I am the pain of the sick,
> I am both cloud and rain, I have rained in the meadows[1].

Now, belief in such a Universal Being need not involve the pantheist's belief that all things are God and that God is all things. The Neoplatonists, with their doctrine of emanation, were theists, although "the One" of Plotinus is not a personal God, and a similar position is reached in some types of mysticism which are not so much religious as philosophical. But the mysticism of Ḥalláj, Ghazálí, Ibnu 'l-Fárid, and Jalálu'ddín Rúmí, like that of all the early Súfís, is predominantly religious. Take a few definitions: "hatred of the world and love of the Lord": "death to self and life in God"; "to form one's self on the character of God." The object of this religious feeling is not a Being without personal attributes but "a personality so wide as to include in itself all existence and all action, all matter and all force[2]." It is at once

[1] *Selected poems from the Díwáni Shamsi Tabríz*, p. 332.
[2] Whinfield, *Masnavi*, p. xix.

universally immanent and absolutely transcendent, and it expresses itself most completely in Man, who is nothing except in so far as he realises his true nature to be the image of the Divine. "The eternal being of God is then that in which ours is rooted, which, since He is before and beyond our individual being, we can worship and love and make the object of our devotion[1]." It is the religious life of the soul, its longing for union with God, and its contemplation of Him in moments of ecstasy, that Jalálu'ddín chiefly dwells on. Any one who is acquainted with the writings of St Teresa, St John of the Cross, and other Christian mystics will easily find parallels to such passages as the following:

O Thou who art my soul's comfort in the season of sorrow,
O Thou who art my spirit's treasure in the bitterness of dearth,
That which the imagination hath not conceived, that which the understanding hath not seen.
Visiteth my soul from Thee, hence in worship I turn toward Thee.

* * * * * *

If a never-ceasing bounty should offer kingdoms,
If a hidden treasure should set before me all that exists,
I would bow down with my soul, I would lay my face in the dust,
I would say, "Of all these the love of such a One for me!"[2]

Usually, as here, the poet turns to God with praise and thanksgiving, but sometimes it is God himself that speaks:

Come, come, for you will not find another friend like me;
Where indeed is a Beloved like me in all the world?
Come, come, and do not spend your life in wandering to and fro,
Since there is no market elsewhere for your money.

[1] Prof C. C. J. Webb, *Problems in the relations of God and Man*, p 281

[2] *Selected poems from the Diwán-i Shamsi Tabríz*, pp 23–24.

You are as a dry valley and I as the rain,
You are as a ruined city and I as the architect.
Except my service, which is joy's sunrise,
Man never has felt and never will feel an impression of joy[1].

The call of the Divine "Thou" to the human "I" implies that the "I" is free to accept or refuse, even though all its actions are ultimately determined by the "Thou." Hence Jalálu'ddín can say:

Thee I *choose*, of all the world, alone;
Wilt Thou suffer me to sit in grief?
My heart is as a pen in Thy hand,
Thou art the cause if I am glad or melancholy.
Save what Thou willest, what will have I?
Save what Thou showest, what do I see?
If Thou keep'st me that, that I am;
If Thou would'st have me this, I am this
In the vessel where Thou givest colour to the soul,
Who am I? What is my love and hate?
When Thou art hidden, I am of the infidels;
When Thou art manifest, I am of the faithful[2].

This brings us to the question of evil, pain, and sin. Jalálu'ddín, as the head of a religious order, had to deal with these matters in a practical way. Like Plotinus, he holds evil in itself to be mere defect and negation—not-being as opposed to Being; but while he knows that it is altogether unreal in relation to God, he is deeply conscious of its reality in relation to man.

"If thou hast not seen the Devil," he exclaims, "look at thyself![3] Be ashamed of thy sins, confess them humbly to God, beseech Him to pardon them and so change thy heart that thou wilt loathe what thou hast done and renounce it utterly."

But why, it may be asked, has God created that to which

[1] *Selected poems from the Díwání Shamsi Tabríz*, p. 179
[2] *Ibid.* p 121
[3] Whinfield, *Masnaví*, p. 51.

men give the name of evil? And since He is the only real Agent, how are we to blame for the actions that we are car to commit? It is characteristic of Jalálu'ddín that he finds the answer to this old riddle not in thought but in feeling, not in theological speculation but in religious experience. We can feel as one what we must think as two Every thing has an opposite by means of which it is manifested; God alone, whose being includes all things, has no opposite, and therefore He remains hidden[1]. Evil is the inevitable condition of good: "out of darkness was created light[2]." From this standpoint it possesses a positive value: it serves the purposes of God, it is relatively good. There is reason as well as rhyme in uniting *ranj*, pain, with *ganj*, gain.

> The prayers of those free from pain are dull and cold,
> The prayers of the sorrowful come from burning hearts[3].

Suffering purifies, sin leads to repentance, and evil is turned to good for the righteous who say like Adam, *Rabbaná ẓalamná anfusaná*, "O Lord, we have done wrong unto our souls[4]."

Answering the Necessitarian argument, Jalálu'ddín insists that our actions, though the effect of Divine agency, are nevertheless freely willed by us, so that we have no right to make God responsible for them. The Divine gift of free will, he says, was refused by the heavens and the earth but was accepted by man at his own peril[5]. It is true that God decrees evil in order that good may be manifested and realised; it is true that in this world the spirit and the flesh are wedded to each other and wage unceasing strife; but it is also true that while the good

[1] Whinfield, *Masnavi*, p 23. [2] *Ibid*. p. 58.
[3] *Ibid*. p. 115. [4] Kor. VII, 22.
[5] Whinfield, *Masnavi*, p. 279.

man accepts evil so far as it is God's ordinance, he does not willingly consent to it so far as it proceeds from his own lusts and passions. Jalálu'ddín would have agreed with Professor Webb in defining sin as "the voluntary surrender of oneself to lower instincts where a different course of action was open[1]." Not that man in the exercise of his will can act at all apart from the will of God, or act well unless he be constantly helped by the grace of God. Spinoza, it will be remembered, taught that "through acquiescence in the universal order based upon knowledge of what it is and what is our place therein we enjoy that liberty which the man who is 'passion's slave' can never have[2]." According to him, real freedom consists in knowledge of the determining causes of our actions. The religious counterpart of this doctrine is Jalálu'ddín's assertion that freedom in the full sense of the term belongs only to the man who *loves* God so perfectly that his will is one with the Divine will: in that unity of feeling the antithesis of freedom and necessity disappears.

The word "compulsion" makes me impatient for Love's sake,
'Tis only he who loves not that is fettered by "compulsion."
This is communion with God, not "compulsion,"
The shining of the moon, not a cloud.
Or if it be "compulsion," it is not ordinary "compulsion,"
It is not the "compulsion" exerted by self-will, inciting us to sin[3].

The man who has thus passed away from his individual self and under the control of God is called by Moslems *walí*, a word which is usually translated in English by "saint." Not all Ṣúfís are saints: the *walís* form a comparatively small class of men and women who have at-

[1] *Problems in the relations of God and Man*, p 118.
[2] *Ibid*. p. 113.
[3] *Masnaví* (Búláq ed.), I, 59.

tained to the highest mystical experience. Their relation to God is such that in them the Divine personality reflects itself and through them is revealed to others. Jalálu'ddín says:

> The mosque that is built in the hearts of the saints
> Is the place of worship for all, for God dwells there[1].

In the *Masnavi* we read how Báyazíd Bisṭámí set out to make the pilgrimage to Mecca and on his way met with the head of the saintly hierarchy, who bade him go no further, saying—

> Of a truth that is God which your soul sees in me,
> For God has chosen me to be His house.
> When you have seen me, you have seen God
> And have circumambulated the real Ka'ba
> To serve me is to worship and praise God;
> Think not that God is distinct from me[2]

The idea of Divine personality is objectified in the perfect saint, whose hand is as the hand of God[3] and by whom the grace of God is dispensed to those who invoke God in his name. Such was the attitude of Jalálu'ddín himself towards his spiritual preceptor, Shamsu'ddín of Tabríz. But every Ṣúfí who adheres to Islam—and for the present we may ignore the wild pantheists and free-thinking dervishes who reject positive religion altogether—must acknowledge that above the saints, even the most perfect of them, stands the Prophet Mohammed. The religious life in Islam could not find its supreme ideal anywhere but in the person of Mohammed. We shall come, therefore, to the heart of our subject if we now proceed to consider what are the relations which Moslems and especially Ṣúfís believe to exist between the Prophet and

[1] Whinfield, *Masnavi*, p. 100 [2] *Ibid.* p. 89.
[3] *Ibid.* p. 46.

God on the one hand and between the Prophet and themselves on the other. If this question had been settled in accordance with the plain meaning of the Koran and the early Traditions, Mohammed, instead of being superior to the Ṣúfistic *walí* and the Shí'ite Imám, would not have been worthy to loose their shoes. Both the *walí* and the Imám are, in a certain sense, *θεῖοι ἄνθρωποι*, divine men, really one with God, whereas Mohammed, as described in the Koran, is no more than a man subject to human weaknesses, who receives at intervals the Divine revelation, not from God but from an angel. He has never seen God, he does not share God's secrets, he cannot foretell the future, he can work no miracle: he is only the servant and messenger of Allah. The historical Prophet was incredible even to his contemporaries. They could not understand him when he disclaimed all supernatural powers, and when he died, 'Umar (who afterwards became Caliph) swore that he was not dead and would assuredly return and cut off the hands and feet of the blasphemers[1]. Such ideas developed rapidly when Islam spread over Western Asia and came into contact with ancient traditions, feelings, and beliefs which it was unable to uproot and which penetrated it in every direction. Under these influences the conception of the Prophet's person was transformed so as to satisfy the religious consciousness. At an early date the dogma of his pre-existence established itself among the Shi'ites, and ere long the Sunnís too adopted it. We find it in many sayings attributed to Mohammed; for example, in the famous Ḥadíth, "I was a prophet whilst Adam was still between the water and the clay," *i.e.* before Adam's body was created. The pre-existent form of Mohammed, which is the first thing that God

[1] Ṭabarí, I, 1815, 14 foll.

created, was conceived as a celestial light: this light (*núr Muḥammadí*) became incarnate in Adam and in the whole series of prophets after him from generation to generation until its final appearance, according to the Sunnís, in Mohammed himself; according to the Shí'ites it passed from Mohammed to 'Alí and the Imáms of his House. The Súfís make use of this doctrine in their own way. By them the Light of Mohammed is identified with the Divine Spirit, which God breathed into Adam, with the Neoplatonic *νοῦς*, which is the first emanation from the One, and with the Logos which, according to some Christian Gnostics, becomes incarnate in the prophets and carries on the cycle of Revelation. The Islamic Logos doctrine, as it may fairly be called, assumes various shapes and is set forth in such a mystical fashion that its details are often difficult to understand. But the main features are clear enough. Mohammed, that is, the essential Idea (*haqíqat*) of Mohammed as opposed to his earthly manifestation, is regarded, firstly, as the centre and animating principle of the whole created universe, the spirit and life of all things, and secondly as the Mediator of Divine grace, the channel through which God imparts knowledge of Himself to his worshippers and endows them with every spiritual gift.

In speaking of Ḥalláj I referred to the tradition, taken over by the Ṣúfís from Judaism, that God created Adam in His own image. Ḥalláj interpreted this as meaning that God manifested Himself in Adam, who objectified the whole Divine nature—both the *láhút* and the *násút*. Ibnu 'l 'Arabí in the 13th century A.D. and 'Abdu 'l-Karím at Jílí in the 14th made the Ḥallájian theory a basis for far-reaching speculations in which the place of Adam is occupied by Mohammed, who, as the Logos, is now identified with the ideal type of humanity, the Perfect Man (ἄνθρωπος τέλειος).

"You must know," says Jílí, "that the Perfect Man is a copy of God That is so because God is Living, Knowing, Mighty, Willing, Hearing, Seeing, and Speaking; and Man too is all these....Further, you must know that the Divine Names and Attributes belong to the Perfect Man by fundamental and sovereign right in virtue of a necessity inherent in his essence, for it is he whose Idea (*ḥaqíqat*) is signified by those expressions and whose spiritual reality is indicated by these symbols they have no subject in existence whereto they should be attached, except the Perfect Man. As a mirror in which a person sees the form of himself and cannot see it without the mirror, such is the relation of God to the Perfect Man, who cannot possibly see his own form but in the mirror of the name Allah; and he is also a mirror to God, for God laid upon Himself the necessity that His Names and Attributes should not be seen save in the Perfect Man[1]."

Hence the Prophet said, or at least is believed by the Ṣúfís to have said, "He that hath seen me hath seen Allah," just as Christ said, "He that hath seen me hath seen the Father."

Moḥammed, then, is not only the source of all the knowledge which the prophets and saints possess concerning God; he himself is the Divine Idea immanent in Creation and the final cause of all that exists, the cosmic thought assuming form and connecting Absolute Being with the world of Nature. He represents the Divine Providence whereby the world is sustained and governed. He is the Khalífat Allah, the Vicegerent of God, the God-Man who has descended to this earthly sphere that he may make manifest the glory of Him who brought the universe into existence. The universe is but the copy of the Idea of Mohammed. even as the Idea of Mohammed

[1] *Studies in Islamic Mysticism*, pp. 106-107.

is the copy of God. The Perfect Man is the microcosm, the universe the macrocosm. Therefore it is appropriate that he should be described in words like these—

All the beauty in the world is borrowed from him and subsists through his beauty and his light. 'Tis his beauty that is beheld in every beauty; 'tis his light that is seen in every light, in the sun, the moon, and the stars. Those who love the Prophet ought to behold his perfection in all that is beautiful and meditate on him, revering him in their hearts and praising him with their tongues I knew one of our Shaykhs who, whenever he saw or thought of anything beautiful, used to cry, "Blessings and peace on thee, O Apostle of God!"[1]

Reference has been made to the belief that the pre-existent Light of Mohammed was revealed in all the prophets from Adam to Jesus and finally manifested in the Seal of the prophets, the last of the whole line, namely, Mohammed himself. His death, however, did not bring the revelation to an end. According to the Ṣúfís, it continues to this day, and those persons who carry on the Prophetic torch are, of course, the *walís* or saints. The relation in which the spiritual adepts of Ṣúfism stand to Mohammed is far closer than that of his most devout and devoted followers amongst the Sunnís, who venerate him as the embodiment of their highest moral and religious ideals. Veneration is not the same thing as love; and love, in the true mystical sense, means that lover and beloved are essentially one. As we have seen, the Ṣúfí saints claim oneness with God, and in this respect they have the closest personal communion with Mohammed, who as the Perfect Man reflecting all the Divine attributes is himself the saint *par excellence*, the absolute type of that peculiar relation to God which the Ṣúfís call *wiláyat*; and

[1] Andrae, *Die Person Muhammeds*, p 354.

it may be added that this inward and saintly aspect of Mohammed's nature is generally regarded by the Ṣúfís as being superior to the outward aspect in which he appears as prophet and apostle. From one point of view, the saints are his personal representatives and vicegerents to whom he has delegated his functions as the Khalífa of God. Without their invisible government the world would fall into disorder and ruin, and without their mediation the Divine blessings would not be dispensed to mankind. Hence they often speak of themselves in terms which would be more suitably applied to God or the Prophetic Logos, but this is not the language of blasphemous arrogance: it is only a tribute to the Divine Being with whom they feel themselves to be one or to the Spirit of Mohammed which lives and works in them. As a rule, the unique pre-eminence of Mohammed is acknowledged even by those Moslem saints who are most conscious of their own deification.

"That which the prophets have," said Báyazíd Bisṭámí, "may be compared to a skin containing honey. A single drop trickles from it, and that drop is the portion of the saints; while to our Prophet—on whom be peace!—belongs all the honey in the skin[1]."

It is true that in the experience of union with God there is no room for a Mediator: here the absolute Divine Unity is realised. And of course we find, especially amongst the ancient Ṣúfís, a feeling that God must be the sole object of adoration, that any regard for other objects is an offence against Him. The woman-saint, Rábi'a of Baṣra, was asked:

"Dost thou love God Almighty?" "Yes." "And dost thou hate the Devil?" "Nay," she replied; "my love of God leaves me no leisure to hate the Devil. I saw the Prophet

[1] Qushayrí, 188, 20.

in a dream. He said, 'O Rábi'a, dost thou love me?' I said, 'O Apostle of God, who does not love thee?—but love of God hath so absorbed me that neither love nor hate of any other thing remains in my heart.'"[1]

To Abú Sa'íd al-Kharráz, however, who also had seen the Prophet in a dream and given the same answer to the same question, Mohammed said, "He that loves God must have loved me[2]"; and later on, when a different view prevailed of the Prophet's relation to God, so that he was identified with the Divine Spirit and with Universal Reason, it became easy to love and worship him without compromising the Unitarian principle. Ghazálí, as I said in my last Lecture, seems to have approached this position in his doctrine of "the Obeyed One" (*al-Muṭá'*). At any rate, during the Middle Ages the Person of Mohammed stands in the very centre of the mystical life of Islam. Abu 'l-Ḥasan al-Ḥirálí, a Ṣúfí of the 13th century, describes three kinds of faith in the Prophet. The third and highest kind is peculiar to those in reference to whom God hath said, "Heaven and earth contain Me not, but the heart of my believing servant containeth Me." They love one another in God and are the vicegerents of God in the world. Their faith consists in the belief that when the Prophet ascended to heaven he received of God's Word (*amr*) that which is hidden from all the prophets and angels and from Gabriel himself. None of the holy spirits and cherubim ever enjoyed such a Divine Revelation as was bestowed on Mohammed. And faith in Mohammed is the measure of one's faith in God. The only way to God is through faith in Mohammed[3]. Here, as Andrae remarks, Mohammed is no more

[1] *Tadhkiratu 'l-Awliyá*, I, 67, 5.
[2] *Ibid.* II, 41, 14.
[3] Andrae, *Die Person Muhammeds*, pp. 310–312.

the Messenger of Allah but the Confidant familiar with Divine mysteries.

> Not the Book, which he has brought, but he himself, his own person, is the Truth and the Guide . . . Faith in him is not a belief in the Prophetic message, but the mystic's personal relation to the Prophet himself the perfect saints are united with him through love and spiritual brotherhood.

The language in which this devotion to the Prophet is expressed often recalls that of erotic hymns to the Deity. He is the Beloved of God (*Ḥabíb Allah*), and therefore the Beloved of all Súfís We hear of mystical union with him, of "passing away" (*faná*) in him. Imitation of his actions and qualities is not enough: his living presence is longed for. Sometimes he assumes the form of a saint and is recognised by the initiated, but it is more usual to see him in dreams. Such visions indeed are a regular feature of the Ṣúfí's experience, and their effect upon his outward and inward life may be momentous. To take one specimen of a type which frequently recurs, it is well known, says Hujwírí, that Junayd of Baghdád refused to discourse on Ṣúfism as long as his spiritual director, Sarí al-Saqaṭí, was alive. One night he dreamed that the Prophet said to him, "O Junayd, speak to the people, for God hath made thy words the means of saving a multitude of mankind." When he awoke, it came into his head that he was superior to Sarí, inasmuch as the Prophet had commanded him to preach. At daybreak, however, Sarí sent a disciple to Junayd with the following message:

> You would not discourse to your disciples when they urged you to do so, and you rejected the intercession of the Shaykhs of Baghdád and my personal entreaty. Now that the Prophet has ordered you, obey his command.

Junayd said,

> I perceived that the rank of Sarí was higher than mine, since he was acquainted with my secret thoughts. I went to him and begged his pardon and asked him how he knew that I had dreamed of the Prophet. He answered, "I dreamed of God, who told me that He had sent the Prophet to bid you preach[1]."

Hujwírí adds the remark that this anecdote clearly indicates that spiritual directors are always acquainted with the inward experiences of their disciples.

Through the mediation of their Prophet the Mohammedan mystics receive guidance in perplexity, aid in misfortune, and comfort in sorrow. But he gives them more than this. On one occasion Abú Ḥamza Baghdádí fell into an ecstasy in which, as he declared, he saw God face to face. His biographer, Farídu'ddín 'Aṭṭár, makes the following comment:

> If such a vision be vouchsafed to any one of the Mohammedan community, it comes not from himself but through the light of the Spirit of Mohammed, on whom be peace. Not that a hundred saints can attain to the rank of the Prophet, but it is in the power of the Prophet to bestow on his community a portion of that which he enjoys, just as Moses caused his people to hear the words which God spoke to him in their presence[2].

Then there is the cardinal matter of intercession for sins. One of the things every Moslem must believe is that the Prophet "will make intercession on the Day of Resurrection in the midst of the Judgment, when we shall stand and long to depart even though it be into the Fire[3]." Though, according to the orthodox, the right of inter-

[1] *Kashf al-Maḥjúb*, transl., p. 129.

[2] *Tadhkiratu 'l-Awliyá*, II, 260, 16–261, 7.

[3] Al-Fuḍálí, translated by D B. Macdonald, *Development of Muslim Theology*, p 349

cession belongs to the Prophet alone, it is claimed by the Ṣúfí saints as part of their heritage from him and they vie with each other in promising forgiveness to all who have loved them and done good work for them, or even seen them. This at least introduces a personal relation between the mediator and the sinner, which in some cases is accompanied by a deep sense of sin. In early Ṣúfism we meet with the pessimistic idea that the amount of sin in the world grows ever greater in proportion to the length of time that has elapsed since the Prophet's decease. One day—so the story is told—Muḥammad ibn 'Alí al-Tirmidhí, who was then an old man, was reviewing his past life. He remembered how once in his youth he had been tempted to sin but had resisted the temptation. He thought to himself, "What if I had yielded to it; for I was young, and I could have repented afterwards." It grieved him bitterly that such a sinful thought should have entered his heart, and for three days he sat plunged in remorse. Then he dreamed that the Prophet came to him and said: "Do not grieve: it is no fault of thine, but forty more years have passed since my death and I am farther away from the world. That is the cause of thy backsliding[1]." A doctrine so unspiritual as this could not satisfy those who sought personal intercourse with the Prophet. "Mohammed is not dead," said Abu 'l-'Abbás al-Qaṣṣáb; "what is dead is thy gift of seeing him with thine inward eye[2]." And how intimately personal are the feelings with which some Islamic mystics regard him you may judge from the following verses written in the 12th century A.D. by Abdu 'l-Raḥím al-Bur'í, a Ṣúfí of Yemen. You will notice, too, that here the Prophet is invoked, not as one whose intercession with God brings

[1] *Tadhkiratu 'l-Awliyá*, II, 94, 24 foll. [2] *Ibid.* II, 185, 8.

about forgiveness of sin, but as one who can himself forgive and take away sin in virtue of the Divine grace and mercy with which he is endowed.

O y Lord, O Apostle of God, O my hope on the day when I shall stand before the Judge!
I beseech thee, by thy glory, to forgive the sins which I have committed, and let thy merit weigh down my scales!
Hearken to my prayer and deliver me from the troubles which have befallen me; comfort me in all my afflictions!
Thou art the nearest in whom we may have hope, albeit thou art far from my house and home
With thee, O son of Abraham, I seek refuge from my sins and trespasses.

* * * * * *

Do thou take my hand, O thou who art quick to answer when I call thee, and graciously pardon me and say,
"To-morrow (on the Day of Judgment) 'Abdu 'l-Raḥím will be my friend." He that is thy friend need not fear he will be lost

* * * * * *

O Lord of the Revelation, there is nothing more precious to me than thy grace.

* * * * * *

I am bound fast in my sins. I who have been conquered and made captive by my sins call unto thee.
Wilt not thou of thy grace set me free? My back is laden with heavy sins, for I have walked in perilous ways in company with sinners.
I have broken my covenant with God. O thou who hast kept thy covenant, turn in compassion and lovingkindness towards 'Abdu 'l-Raḥím![1]

It must have occurred to many of you that the ideas which we have been discussing—the ideas developed in later Ṣúfism concerning the person of Mohammed—show a remarkable likeness to what is known in Christian theology as the doctrine of a Mediator. I am not qualified

[1] Andrae, *Die Person Muhammeds*, p. 389.

to speak with any authority on the subject, but in order to bring out some points of resemblance and difference between Christian and Islamic conceptions of personality, I may quote part of the explanation given by Professor Webb, from whose books I have already drawn a good deal of interesting matter. In Christianity, he says, the Mediator is the Son of God, in whom, according to St Paul, "dwelleth all the fullness of the Godhead bodily."

> The thought of St Paul...seems to be that the longer and inclusive life in which that of any individual man or woman must find its completion is the life of God...yet it can only find this completion in the divine life when that life is poured out, so to say, into a person who, while thus sharing the divine nature, is yet distinguished from God. The distinction from God which Religion implies remains to the end; but the difference of the created nature from the divine is transcended through the intimate union (symbolised by that of the members of a body with its head) with a Spirit essentially one with God, though distinguishable from him, the archetype of the created spirits, who obtain in their union with this Spirit what is described as a sonship, not, like that Spirit's own, by nature, but by adoption[1].

The facts of religious experience (he goes on to say)

> will be found to involve, when worked into a theological doctrine, the recognition of a twofold Personality in the Divine Nature. For we have to express a consciousness of personal communion with God felt on the one hand to be a communion of spirit with kindred spirit, of Son with Father, and yet on the other to belong as such not to the individual in isolation and imperfection but in the ideal and archetype of his nature....Here the personal communion itself, as belonging to the true nature of God—and in nothing less than this can the aspiration of the religious consciousness find satisfaction—implies a personal distinction within that

[1] *God and Personality*, p. 166.

nature; while the individual further distinguishes his own separate and imperfect personality from the ideal personality which is thought of as eternally distinguishing itself from God in the communion which is the consummation of the religious life[1]

There are obvious reasons why no similar development of the Idea of Personality could have been reached in Islam. In the first place, it is impossible for any Moslem to conceive the relationship between God and man as that of Father and Son Allah is the Creator; and though the metaphor of "creation," which implies His transcendence, is often exchanged for "emanation," which implies His immanence, yet all beings, including Mohammed himself, are on one side of their nature His creatures, His slaves, absolutely inferior to Him. And Allah in His essence is One. In His essence there can be no interplay of personality. The Islamic conception of plurality in the Divine Unity signifies not the relation of persons within that Unity, but the relations existing between that Unity and the manifold aspects in which it reveals itself. All these aspects are reflected in the Perfect Man, who may therefore be described as the personified Idea in and through whom the Divine nature makes itself known While the Christian doctrine expresses "the realisation of human personality as characterised by and consummated in the indwelling reality of the Spirit of Christ, which is God[2]," in Mohammedan theology the main stress falls on Revelation. In Islam the oldest form of the Logos doctrine is impersonal. The Logos is represented by the Koran, the eternal Word of Allah. "This, it may be said roughly, is our Nicene form of the Logos doctrine. On

[1] *God and Personality*, p 182

[2] R. C. Moberly, cited by Rufus Jones, *Studies in mystical religion*, Introd, p. xvi.

the other hand, the Arian form appears in the doctrine of the person of Mohammed. He is the first of created beings and for his sake the worlds were created[1]." But the worlds were created in order that God might be known, and the Perfect Man is pre-eminently the Mediator through whom all knowledge of God is revealed. You will recollect that the religious life of the Súfí culminates in knowledge of God, gnosis (*ma'rifat*). Professor Browne, speaking of the Ismá'ílís, has admirably explained this point of view.

"The truth is," he writes, "that there is a profound difference between the Persian idea of Religion and that which obtains in the West. Here it is the ideas of Faith and Righteousness (in different proportions, it is true) which are regarded as the essentials of Religion; there it is Knowledge and Mystery. Here Religion is regarded as a rule by which to live and a hope wherein to die; there as a Key to unlock the Secrets of the Spiritual and Material Universe. Here it is associated with Work and Charity; there with Rest and Wisdom[2]."

The contrast, however, must not be pressed too far. In the present course of Lectures some examples have been given—and their number might easily be increased—of experiences and feelings of faith, love, and devotion which are entirely religious in the sense attached to the word by Christians. The Ṣúfí who would know God must first be made pure in heart. Journeying along this path he sees before him the figure of Mohammed—"poor, humble, self-abasing, misunderstood by the world, mild, forgiving, compassionate to all." It may be, says Andrae, that the character of the Prophet, as depicted by the Ṣúfís, represents the moral ideal of the East—an ideal which

[1] D. B. Macdonald, in *Vital forces of Christianity and Islam* (Oxford, 1915), p. 228.

[2] *Literary History of Persia*, vol. I, p. 405.

seems to have been powerfully influenced by its embodiment in the person of Christ. "And indeed," he adds, "the ethics of Ṣúfism would appear to be more akin than any other system of morality to the Sermon on the Mount[1]."

There are, of course, many aspects of our subject which I have left untouched, either from want of time or because they could not be treated adequately by one who has had no special training in philosophy. I should have liked, for instance, to show you how the idea of personality in Ṣúfism is fostered by the intensely and peculiarly personal intercourse of the Ṣúfís with each other. The closeness of the tie between *Shaykh* and *murid*, teacher and disciple, is almost proverbial—the *murid* is called the son of the Shaykh—and apart from this unique relation every disciple has his own little group of intimate friends, to whom he is a centre, so to speak, of psychological interest, who share his thoughts and feelings and enter with sympathy into all that concerns him[2]. Further, the whole Ṣúfí community forms one indivisible brotherhood, so that the meanest famulus feels himself to be joined in spirit with the most exalted hierophant. The Ṣúfís look upon themselves as God's chosen people, loved by Him and loving one another in Him; and the bond between them can never be broken, for it is a marriage of true souls, which was made in Heaven. This is what Abu Sa'íd ibn Abi 'l-Khayr says in the following passage:

Four thousand years before God created these bodies, He created the souls and kept them beside Himself and shed a light upon them. He knew what quantity of light each soul

[1] Andrae, *Die Person Muhammeds*, pp. 227 fol.
[2] *Ibid.* pp. 367 foll.

received and He was showing favour to each in proportion to its illumination. The souls remained all that time in the light until they became fully nourished. Those who in this world live in joy and agreement with one another must have been akin to one another in yonder place. Here they love another and are called the friends of God, and they are brethren who love one another for God's sake. These souls know each other by the smell, like horses Though one be in the East and the other in the West, yet they feel joy and comfort in each other's talk, and one who lives in a later generation than the other is instructed and consoled by the words of his friend[1].

In an atmosphere thus charged with personal forces and influences we find, as might be expected, great emphasis laid on the survival of personality after death and on intercourse with the spirits of those who have passed away. The literature of Ṣúfism furnishes innumerable testimonies that deceased saints are seen in dreams, relate what has happened to them in the next world, and speak words of counsel, encouragement, or reproof to their friends living on earth. It may be said, I think, that many Ṣúfís have held a doctrine resembling that of Ibn Síná (Avicenna) as to the immortality of the individual soul and its union—but not its complete unification—with the World-Spirit, such union constituting the blessedness of the good[2]. Others, again, seem to regard "absorption in the Deity, the merging of the individual soul of the saint in the Universal Soul of God," as the ideal which, though temporarily attainable in this life, only receives permanent realisation in another state of existence. Ibn Síná, Ibnu 'l-Fáriḍ, and Jalálu'ddín Rúmí reject the doctrine of transmigration of souls (*tanásukh*), but Jalálu'ddín teaches that as man has risen from inanimate

[1] *Studies in Islamic Mysticism*, p. 56.
[2] T. J. de Boer, *The History of Philosophy in Islam*, pp. 142 fol.

matter, through the vegetable and animal worlds, to the stage of humanity, so after death he will continue his spiritual evolution and become an angel in heaven. But this is not the end. "Pass on even from angelhood," says the poet; "enter that Sea, that your drop of water may become a boundless ocean[1]." These words can only mean, I take it, that human personality is a transient phenomenon which ultimately disappears in what alone is real—the eternal and everlasting Personality of God.

So we come back to the point from which we started, to the absolute unity and transcendence of the Divine nature. It is very curious that notwithstanding the strength and depth of the personal relations which, as we have seen, unite Ṣúfís with each other, with the Prophetic Mediator, and with God Himself, these relations so often appear to reach their climax in a unity which excludes all relations—the unity of the rain-drop lost in the ocean or of the moth consumed in the flame of the candle[2]. I do not know how to explain this, and certainly the word "pantheism" does not give a satisfactory explanation of it. Any attempt at a solution would have to begin, I think, by recognising that the Moslem's conception of personality is different from ours. In Islam God, not man, is the measure of all things. In Islam there has hitherto been no place for what we call Humanism, implying the value and sufficiency of the individual as such. In Islam the Perfect Man, who is identified with Mohammed, represents the idea of Divinity revealing itself in man rather than the ideal of Humanity realising itself in the personal

[1] *Selected poems from the Díwáni Shamsi Tabríz*, pp. 47–48. Cf. Whinfield, *Masnaví*, p. 159.

[2] The burnt moth, however, is used by Ḥalláj as an emblem of the sublimated personality of the saint united with God (*Tawásín*, pp. 16 fol.).

life of God. Hence it is not surprising that the experiences of the Ṣúfís should lack the psychological richness and variety which is to be found in Western mysticism. Still, they are interesting, as I hope the slight account of them given in these Lectures may have shown; and in any case they must be studied because of the light they shed on the ways in which Moslems think of the great mysteries of life and religion.

INDEX